WHAT IS CANADA?
The Ultimate Canadian Quiz Book

© 2008 by Blue Bike Books
First printed in 2008 10 9 8 7 6 5 4 3 2 1
Printed in Canada

All rights reserved. No part of this work covered by the copyrights hereon may be reproduced or used in any form or by any means—graphic, electronic or mechanical—without the prior written permission of the publisher, except for reviewers, who may quote brief passages. Any request for photocopying, recording, taping or storage on information retrieval systems of any part of this work shall be directed in writing to the publisher.

The Publisher: Blue Bike Books
Website: www.bluebikebooks.com

Library and Archives Canada Cataloguing in Publication

De Figueiredo, Dan, 1964-
   What is Canada? : the ultimate Canadian quiz book / Dan de Figueiredo.

ISBN 13: 978-1-897278-50-5
ISBN 10: 1-897278-50-0

   1. Canada—Miscellanea. I. Title.

FC60.D253 2008   971   C2008-902832-5

Project Director: Nicholle Carrière
Project Editor: Kathy van Denderen
Production: Jodene Draven
Cover Images: 2008 Jupiterimages Corporation; Elena Elisseeva | Dreamstime.com
Illustrations: Pat Bidwell, Roger Garcia, Patrick Hénaff, Graham Johnson, Peter Tyler, Roly Wood

We acknowledge the support of the Alberta Foundation for the Arts for our publishing program.

PC: P5

WHAT IS CANADA?

The Ultimate Canadian Quiz Book

Dan de Figueiredo

BLUE BIKE BOOKS

CONTENTS

INTRODUCTION 7
CHAPTER 1:   Canada Today 9
CHAPTER 2:   Quotations to Inspire a Nation 19
CHAPTER 3:   Canadian Emblems, Holidays and Observances. . 31
CHAPTER 4:   The Pre-Confederation History of Canada 59
CHAPTER 5:   The Education of a Canadian, along with
             Uniquely Canadian Words. 85
CHAPTER 6:   Professional Sports of the Canadian Variety . . . 123
CHAPTER 7:   Canadian Geography with Some Oddities
             Thrown in for Good Measure 149
CHAPTER 8:   Canadian Wildlife, Environment and Weather. . 183
CHAPTER 9:   Canada's Military History 203
CHAPTER 10: Amateur and Olympic Sports. 227
CHAPTER 11: Science, Industry, Invention—and the Greats
            Involved in Each! 253
CHAPTER 12: Art, Literature and Entertainment 275
CHAPTER 13: The Dark Side—Crime, Criminals, Misdeeds
            and Much More! 317
CHAPTER 14: The First Nations 349
CHAPTER 15: The Post-Confederation History of Canada. . . . 367
NOTES ON SOURCES 387

DEDICATION

For all those who struggle with the quiz of life...
Always remember...
The answers are in the questions...
Living is in the metaphor...
Nitrates are in bacon, but oh they are sooo good!

But mostly this is for Paul and Simon...
But not as afterthoughts...Really!

INTRODUCTION & ACKNOWLEDGEMENTS

It was, I suppose, inevitable that I would write a quiz-based book. For years I worked in the television industry as a writer and producer of quiz shows. From *TimeChase* (for History Television and Super People Productions) to *Today's the Day* (CBC), *Who Wants To Be a Millionaire* Canadian Edition (CTV), *Reach for the Top* (TVO) and *Inside the Box* (TVtropolis and Lone Eagle). I worked on other shows as well in that medium, but I found myself pegged as the "Quiz Show Guy," though since then I have been able to convince people I am capable of other things.

"Trivia," as I learned in my first job as a writer of "such" things for television, is a bad word. For that matter, "trivia show" and "game show" are bad phrases as well. It's a quiz, a quiz show, and the information and questions therein are not trivia, nor trivial. They are facts. And that my dear friends is what you will find in this book. Questions and answers based on facts, not trivia.

A great many people have guided me through what "makes" a good quiz, and I would like to thank them for their guidance. Sidney Cohen, that master of the Canadian quiz show, was my first guide in the game. He hired me to write for his excellent history quiz show, *TimeChase*. He was the one who took the time to show me how it was all done, from his perspective, of course…. But he was right on, all knowing and always generously telling me about the essential make-up of a successful quiz show.

I worked for Steve Glassman on a show called *Today's the Day*. It never actually saw the light of day in terms of actually being produced into a finished product, despite us working on it over a two-year span of time at the mother corp, CBC. It was a hoot and a half and a paying one at that. And thusly I have nothing but good memories and experiences from that show. Working at CBC was a goldmine, paywise, as well.

Who Wants to Be a Millionaire was a great leap forward for me... I was back in charge (and I like that) of writing and researching, and I learned so much more on that one. Pilot Peppler taught me all about the database, but Ann Miller-George, the supervising producer of the American version of *Millionaire,* and her team, showed CTV how it was really done. And how to get the best work in limited time in a pressure cooker. They had a whole floor for the writers and researchers on Park Avenue in New York, stocked with books, research materials, a gym across the street with a paid membership for everyone and snacks ta boot! We, working on the Canadian version of the show, were stuffed into two rooms in a converted garage at gorgeous Channel 9 Court in the wilds of Scarborough, overlooking Highway 401. Though to be fair, we didn't see the highway because our workroom was windowless. And as our team leader once announced on entering these two small rooms stuffed with 16 people, "It stinks in here!" Boy, she was a great help. CTV certainly didn't splurge on offices, research materials or pay, but they had a huge marketing budget and that was what was, and I think still is, important to them.

But let me get back to Ann Miller-George. She left me with this unforgettable phrase: "Pegged correctly"! It has stuck with me ever since. Each question has to be pegged correctly. What does that mean? It means that each and every question has to be written in such a way that there can only be one true answer. This is the Holy Grail that we seek in writing quiz questions. Enough information must be included in each question so that ABSOLUTELY no other answer could ever be correct. I check this idea against all quizzes I read. Most quizzes fail this test.

The other thing you should be aware of is that every word means something. The questions are written to give you clues to the answers, so read with care. "What" and "which" especially are words to watch.

I have tried my darndest to make sure all the questions are pegged correctly. I hope I have succeeded, and that you enjoy my efforts to their fullest.

CANADA TODAY

By way of easing you into the quiz questions, I thought I'd take it easy on you by challenging you to answer a few questions that deal with the most recent of recently current events. So get your pens out (or pencils if you're scared) and move ahead, gentle reader. This first, short quiz should make you smile...and make you feel smart. The tough questions will follow, of course!

1. **Who was sworn in as Canada's 27th governor general in September 2005?**
   A. Adrienne Clarkson
   B. Jeanne Sauvé
   C. Michaëlle Jean

2. **What is the official title of the person who presides over the House of Commons?**
   A. Moderator
   B. Speaker (of the House)
   C. Whip

3. **What is the official name of the upper house of Canada's Parliament?**
   A. The Senate
   B. The Sleeping Chamber
   C. The Red Room

4. **On February 5, 2008, which prime minister's signature sold for $7850 on eBay?**
   A. Sir Robert Borden
   B. Sir John A. Macdonald
   C. Sir Wilfrid Laurier

Answers 1–4

1. C. Michaëlle Jean

2. B. The Speaker (of the House)

3. A. The Senate

4. B. Sir John A. Macdonald

Jason Kelly, a hotel general manager in Ottawa, was the winning bidder of a card that reads "Yours Faithfully, John A. Macdonald." It is an unconfirmed signature, though the buyer said he compared it to verified signatures of Sir John A. and was satisfied that it is authentic. In the last three minutes of the online auction, the bidding jumped from $4601 to the final sale price of $7850. The seller of the card was a former real estate agent from Worcester, Massachusetts, named Patti Kelley.

Questions 5 – 8

5. Within the federal government, which body has exclusive jurisdiction over legislation relating to the raising or spending of money?
   A. The Senate
   B. The House of Commons
   C. The Supreme Court

6. What was the value of the settlement Maher Arar reached with the Canadian government in January 2007 after the RCMP admitted they released misleading evidence to the United States resulting in Arar's deportation and torture in Syria?
   A. $1 million
   B. $10 million
   C. $100 million

7. What Canadian company was involved in a tainted pet food scandal and recall in March 2007 that may have resulted in the deaths of more than 3000 dogs and cats in North America?
   A. Billboard Foods
   B. Snappy Crappy Foods
   C. Menu Foods

8. In October 2007, at what airport did the RCMP stun a Polish traveller with a Taser, resulting in his death?
   A. Vancouver International Airport
   B. Toronto Pearson International Airport
   C. Montréal Mirabel International Airport

WHAT IS CANADA?

ANSWERS 5 – 8

5. B. The House of Commons

6. B. $10 million

7. C. Menu Foods

8. A. Vancouver International Airport

Robert Dziekanski was held up at customs for some 10 hours. The RCMP said he was acting irrationally and was shocked by RCMP Tasers at least twice before being handcuffed on the floor, going into cardiac arrest and dying.

Questions 9–12

9. What hockey player was named Canada's top athlete of the year in 2007?

A. Sidney Crosby
B. Josh Lucas
C. Marc Lalonde

10. In 2007, what former TV reporter was sworn in as Ontario's first lieutenant-governor with a physical disability?

A. James Bartleman
B. Hilary Weston
C. David Onley

11. What Grammy Award–winning jazz pianist and vocalist, nicknamed the "maharaja of the keyboard" by Duke Ellington, passed away at his Mississauga home on December 23, 2007?

A. Dizzy Gillespie
B. Oscar Peterson
C. Jeff Healey

12. In what month in 2007 did Canada's dollar finally reach parity with the U.S. dollar, a mark it last saw in November 1976?

A. July
B. September
C. October

ANSWERS 9 – 12

9. A. Sidney Crosby
He is the captain of the Pittsburgh Penguins.

10. C. David Onley
For many years he worked at Toronto's City TV.

11. B. Oscar Peterson

12. B. September

QUESTIONS 13 – 16

13. In what province did Dalton McGuinty's Liberals win a massive majority in the general election in October 2007?
   A. Ontario
   B. Nova Scotia
   C. Manitoba

14. In what province did the electorate return Ed Stelmach's Progressive Conservative government to power in an election decided on March 3, 2008?
   A. British Columbia
   B. Alberta
   C. Manitoba

15. In July 2007, Canada's national crime rate was reported to be the lowest in how many years?
   A. 10 years
   B. 25 years
   C. 50 years

16. In June 2007, a Vancouver hospital patient was seen to ooze blood of what unexpected colour?
   A. Green
   B. Purple
   C. Orange

Answers 13–16

13. A. Ontario

14. B. Alberta

15. B. 25 years

16. A. Green

It was later determined that nothing was wrong with the man's blood (nor was he of Vulcan origin); instead, his migraine medication had caused the odd colouring of his blood.

Questions 17–20

17. In January 2008, what former Liberal Cabinet minister supplied a report to the Tory government in Ottawa about Canadian military operations in Afghanistan?
    A. Sheila Copps
    B. Paul Martin
    C. John Manley

18. Previously the vice chief of defence staff, who succeeded General Rick Hillier as Canada's chief of defence staff in 2008?
    A. Walter Natynczyk
    B. Peter MacKay
    C. Andrew McNaughton

19. In 2008, which of the following cities celebrate the 400th anniversary of its founding by Europeans?
    A. Montréal
    B. Québec City
    C. St. John's

20. Which "royal" museum was established in 1914, and in 2007 unveiled an angular addition to its structure by architect Daniel Libeskind?
    A. Royal Tyrrell Museum
    B. Royal Ontario Museum
    C. Royal British Columbia Museum

ANSWERS 17–20

17. C. John Manley

18. A. Walter Natyncyk

Walter Natyncyk succeeded Hillier in the top military job on July 1, 2008, when Hillier stepped down.

19. B. Québec City

20. B. Royal Ontario Museum

The addition to the museum was apparently inspired by a crystal and is called The Michael Lee-Chin Crystal and named after the major donor to the project.

QUOTATIONS TO INSPIRE A NATION

All those words and phrases and speeches that become quotable quotations should, I think, inspire, inform, enliven, lift and also on occasion grow to become ironic with time. So test your mettle with these quotable quiz quotations from the famous, used to be famous, infamous and inspired.

21. On January 27, 1996, which provincial premier said, "Canada is divisible because it is not a real country"?
    A. Jacques Parizeau
    B. Lucien Bouchard
    C. Ralph Klein

22. Which wartime prime minister originated the quotation, "Not necessarily conscription, but conscription if necessary"?
    A. William Lyon Mackenzie King
    B. Sir Robert Borden
    C. Stephen Harper

23. Whose report on the rebellion in 1837 contained the phrase, "I expected to find a contest between a government and a people; I found two nations warring in the bosom of a single state"?
    A. John Graves Simcoe
    B. William Lyon Mackenzie
    C. Lord Durham

Answers 21–23

21. B. Lucien Bouchard

Bouchard made the assertion two days before he was sworn in as Parti Québécois premier of Québec. His claim led to many an English Canadian writer claiming that if Canada was divisible, then so was Québec. The back and forth dialogue continued…Tut, tut, tut!

22. A. William Lyon Mackenzie King

Fearing a split along French-English lines during the conscription crisis of World War II, the shrewd Mackenzie King came up with the slogan in an attempt to placate both sides, but if necessary gave the federal government the right to enlist a draft for overseas service in the military. In a national plebiscite, most provinces voted overwhelmingly (80 percent) in favour of the draft. However, in Québec, the vote was the complete opposite, with almost 73 percent opposing conscription. Less than 3000 conscripts actually saw combat in Europe during that war.

23. C. Lord Durham

Questions 24–26

24. Which French Canadian prime minister said during a general election, "In Québec I am branded as a Jingo, and in Ontario as a Separatist. I am neither, I am a Canadian"?

   A. Pierre Trudeau
   B. Sir Wilfrid Laurier
   C. Jean Chrétien

25. During which prime minister's tenure was the Canadian Bill of Rights passed, containing the following phrases: "I am a Canadian, a free Canadian, free to speak without fear… This heritage of freedom I pledge to uphold for myself and all mankind"?

   A. John Diefenbaker
   B. Lester B. Pearson
   C. Pierre Trudeau

26. Which prime minister said, "Americans should never underestimate the constant pressure on Canada which the mere presence of the United States has produced. We're different people from you and we're different people because of you. Living next to you is in some ways like sleeping with an elephant. No matter how friendly and even-tempered is the beast, if I may call it that, one is affected by every twitch and grunt. It should not therefore be expected that this kind of nation, this Canada, should project itself as a mirror image of the United States"?

   A. Louis St. Laurent
   B. Sir Wilfrid Laurier
   C. Pierre Trudeau

ANSWERS 24–26

24. B. Sir Wilfrid Laurier

25. A. John Diefenbaker

The entire quote comes from the 1960 Bill of Rights and reads thusly:

> *I am a Canadian,*
> *free to speak without fear,*
> *free to worship in my own way,*
> *free to stand for what I think right,*
> *free to oppose what I believe wrong,*
> *or free to choose those*
> *who shall govern my country.*
> *This heritage of freedom*
> *I pledge to uphold*
> *for myself and all mankind.*

26. C. Pierre Trudeau

Questions 27–30

27. What author of the children's story *The Secret World of Og* (1961) is also credited with originating the quotation, "A Canadian is someone who knows how to make love in a canoe"?
    A. Mordecai Richler
    B. Pierre Berton
    C. Robert Munsch

28. What wacky BC premier once said, "Let's cut down the trees and create jobs"?
    A. William Vander Zalm
    B. Bill Bennett
    C. Rita Johnston

29. Which Canadian author created the character Sam Slick and is credited with the quotation, "Hope is a pleasant acquaintance, but an unsafe friend"?
    A. Thomas Chandler Haliburton
    B. Stephen Leacock
    C. Lucy Maud Montgomery

30. In the House of Commons in 1985, what MP said, "I am 32 years old, I am an elected Member of Parliament from Hamilton East, and I'm nobody's baby"?
    A. Deborah Grey
    B. Ellen Fairclough
    C. Sheila Copps

Answers 27 – 30

27. B. Pierre Berton

The Secret World of Og was written by Berton in 1961 and illustrated by his daughter Patsy. In 2006, the CBC turned the story into a 26-episode animated series. The infamous quote, "A Canadian is someone who knows how to make love in a canoe," is, according to the *Penguin Dictionary of Popular Canadian Quotations,* attributed to an interview Berton gave to Dick Brown in *The Canadian* on December 22, 1973.

28. A. William Vander Zalm

29. A. Thomas Chandler Haliburton

Haliburton was an immensely popular humorist who wrote the Sam Slick series of books. In the 1830s and 1840s, those books popularized the phrases "it's raining cats and dogs," "quick as a wink" and "facts are stranger than fiction."

30. C. Sheila Copps

The quotation comes from a rather raucous exchange between Copps (then part of the infamous Liberal "Rat Pack") and Justice Minister John Crosbie. Crosbie began by saying, "Just quieten down, baby. You bunch of poltroons can shout all you like. The rat pack can quieten down. The titmice can quieten down." Later, in 1986, Sheila Copps published her autobiography, which she titled *Nobody's Baby* (By the way, Ms. Copps is from my hometown, Hamilton, Ontario, where opinion stands firm that her father, Vic Copps, was a pretty darn good mayor. As for Sheila, well, opinion has always been mixed on what she is good at. And that is all I am saying on that!)

QUOTATIONS TO INSPIRE A NATION

QUESTIONS 31–33

31. What British-born Canadian writer and naturalist is credited with the following quotation, which in the light of events now, seems ironic, "Behind me I had the power of 10,000 miles of wilderness, trees that have never told a lie, though some of them have stood for 2000 years"?
   A. David Suzuki
   B. Conrad Black
   C. Archibald Belaney

32. Which Canadian author is credited with this statement: "We Canadians, as I wrote in the *Spectator* years ago, are the English-speaking world's elected squares. To the British, we are the nicest, whitest Americans. To Americans, we represent a nostalgia for the unhurried horse and buggy age"?
   A. Mordecai Richler
   B. Daniel Richler
   C. Gabrielle Roy

33. What Montréal-born poet and songwriter summed up his idea of a hero thusly: "What I consider a hero is a guy who goes to work every day and supports his family. The ordinary guy. I think to hold it together nowadays is a heroic enterprise"?
   A. Archibald Lampman
   B. Margaret Atwood
   C. Leonard Cohen

Answers 31–33

31. C. Archibald Belaney

Belaney was of course known more famously as Grey Owl. As Grey Owl, he lived the life of an Aboriginal and dressed the part as well. He grew his hair long and wore Native clothing. Belaney claimed his father was Scottish and his mother was Apache. He was an eloquent speaker who made numerous lecture tours across North America and, to his credit, wrote books on the need to preserve the forests, wildlife and Native culture. It was only discovered after his death in 1938 that he was in fact an Englishman, born in Hastings.

32. A. Mordecai Richler

33. C. Leonard Cohen

Questions 34–36

34. Which journalist, author and social activist is credited with saying, "The beaver, which has come to represent Canada as the eagle does the United States and the lion Britain, is a flat-tailed, slow-witted, toothy rodent known to bite off its own testicles or to stand under its own falling trees"?
    A. David Suzuki
    B. June Callwood
    C. Naomi Klein

35. Which Canadian athlete said, "I skate the way I think Isadora Duncan danced. I'm trying to explore every facet of my personality. I'm criticized as flamboyant, arrogant and melodramatic. I'm black and white. I'm yes and no. I try to live my life touching extremes"?
    A. Barbara Ann Scott
    B. Guy Lafleur
    C. Toller Cranston

36. Who campaigned against Free Trade, saying, "Canada, having once become the commercial and industrial vassal of the United States, would inevitably become the political vassal of that country and ultimately be absorbed"?
    A. Sir Wilfrid Laurier
    B. Sir Robert Borden
    C. Jean Chrétien

WHAT IS CANADA?

Answers 34 – 36

34. B. June Callwood

35. C. Toller Cranston

36. B. Sir Robert Borden

Quotations to Inspire a Nation

Questions 37 – 39

37. On September 8, 1939, who cast the sole dissenting vote against Canada declaring war on Germany and said, "I know that truth is one of the first victims of war"?

   A. Tommy Douglas
   B. Arthur Meighen
   C. J.S. Woodsworth

38. What man of letters wrote, "One disadvantage of living in Canada is that one is continually called upon to make statements about the Canadian identity, and Canadian identity is an eminently exhaustible subject"?

   A. Mordecai Richler
   B. Peter C. Newman
   C. Northrop Frye

39. What Canadian entertainer is quoted as saying, "I really feel like life will dictate itself. You should allow it to unfold as naturally as possible. Just go with the flow. When you're really desperate, you say a few prayers and hope for the best. That's the way I've always lived my life"?

   A. Shania Twain
   B. Gordon Lightfoot
   C. Marie Dressler

ANSWERS 37–39

37. C. J.S. Woodsworth

A lifelong pacifist, Woodsworth held firm to his beliefs that Canada should stay neutral in World War II. He was at odds with most of Canada on this issue, including his own party, the Co-operative Commonwealth Federation. In his House of Commons speech opposing the war, he also made this eloquent appeal:

> *I rejoice that it is possible to say these things in a Canadian parliament under British institutions. It would not be possible in Germany, I recognize that...and I want to maintain the very essence of our British institutions of real liberty. I believe that the only way to do it is by an appeal to the moral forces which are still resident among our people, and not by another resort to brute force.*

38. C. Northrop Frye

39. A. Shania Twain

This singer of note from Timmins also once said in a song that rocket scientists didn't impress her much. Philosopher indeed!

CANADIAN EMBLEMS, HOLIDAYS AND OBSERVANCES

There are a great many things that "say" or even perhaps "scream" Canada. In this quizzically quizzical chapter, see if you can figure out which questions are most Canadian. It's a judgement call, I know, but heck, I give you permission, judge away! And by the way, this chapter doesn't just include questions about emblems and holidays, but also people, places, abbreviations, institutions and offices, and officers of note.

40. Which Canadian holiday always falls on the second Monday in October?
    A. Thanksgiving
    B. Remembrance Day
    C. Labour Day

41. Which battlefield memorial to Canadian soldiers lies 10 kilometres north of Arras, France, overlooks the Douai Plain and was designed by Walter Seymour Allward?
    A. Vimy Ridge Memorial
    B. Bourlon Wood Memorial
    C. Passchendaele Memorial

42. In which month did Chinese Canadians celebrate their new year in 2008?
    A. January
    B. February
    C. March

Answers 40–42

40. A. Thanksgiving

41. A. Vimy Ridge Memorial

Walter Allward's design for the Vimy Ridge Memorial was chosen over 160 others. Work began on the monument in 1925, and it was finally unveiled by King Edward VII on July 26, 1936. The Vimy memorial has often been called Canada's most impressive tribute overseas. The monument sits atop the highest point of Vimy Ridge, and the 100 hectares that surround it were given to Canada by France in 1922 in gratitude for sacrifices made by Canada in World War I and more specifically for Canadian soldiers who captured Vimy Ridge in 1917. The following words appear in French and English on the base of the memorial:

> *To the valour of their*
> *Countrymen in the Great War*
> *And in memory of their sixty*
> *Thousand dead this monument*
> *Is raised by the people of Canada*

42. B. February

The first day of the Chinese New Year in 2008 was February 7. According to the Chinese calendar, the year is 4705 and is based upon the movement of the sun, moon and stars. It's the Year of the Rat!...Not a dirty rat, see?

CANADIAN EMBLEMS, HOLIDAYS AND OBSERVANCES

Questions 43 – 47

43. What is the address of the official residence of Canada's prime minister?
   A. 7 Rideau Gate
   B. 24 Sussex Drive
   C. 8 Rockliffe Park

44. What day is celebrated in Québec on June 24?
   A. Canada Day
   B. Bastille Day
   C. St. Jean Baptiste Day

45. What vegetable delicacy is a member of the fern family and has a celebration designated in its honour each May in Rogersville, New Brunswick?
   A. Peat moss
   B. Brussels sprouts
   C. Fiddleheads

46. Which city hosted the 1967 World's Fair, entitled Man and His World?
   A. Montréal
   B. Vancouver
   C. Hamilton

47. Which western province has the wild rose as its floral emblem?
   A. Alberta
   B. Saskatchewan
   C. British Columbia

Answers 43–47

43. B. 24 Sussex Drive
The residence at 24 Sussex Drive was built between 1866 and 1868 by lumberman and member of Canada's first Parliament, William Edwards. It was acquired by the Government of Canada in 1943.

44. C. St. Jean Baptiste Day
Actually, French Canadians all across Canada celebrate St. Jean Baptiste Day, and many people of other ethnicities celebrate along with them. It combines the rites of the summer solstice with the traditional celebration in honour of the patron saint of French Canadians. By the way, Pope Pius X designated St. Jean Baptiste the patron saint of French Canadians in 1908.

45. C. Fiddleheads
Each May, St. Mary's First Nations celebrates the fiddlehead. That's right, those highly perishable, young fronds of the ostrich fern. The fiddlehead is a symbol of the Wolastoqiyik people along the St. John River. The Fiddlehead Festival includes a whole lot of eating of the said fiddleheads, along with a fiddlehead dance, great moments in fiddlehead history and fiddlehead stories.

46. A. Montréal

47. A. Alberta

CANADIAN EMBLEMS, HOLIDAYS AND OBSERVANCES

Questions 48–51

48. In which city would you find the second official home of the governor general of Canada?

   A. Ottawa
   B. Montréal
   C. Québec City

49. In what Ontario town is there a festival celebrating Groundhog Day and featuring a white groundhog named Willie?

   A. Woodstock
   B. Winona
   C. Wiarton

50. Which prime minister saw the adoption of the current Canadian flag?

   A. John Diefenbaker
   B. Lester B. Pearson
   C. Pierre Trudeau

51. Although it's not a national holiday, what February date has been designated Canada's national flag day?

   A. February 1
   B. February 15
   C. February 21

Answers 48–51

48. C. Québec City

The Citadelle was built between 1820 and 1831. The British occupied it until 1871, when the Canadian government finally took it over…peacefully, of course. The governor general's residence at the Citadelle of Québec has been the second official home of every governor general since 1872. It's located in the heart of Québec City's historic quarter and is open to the public for guided tours. In 1872 Lord Dufferin moved into the quarters at the Citadelle and thus established it as the traditional residence for the governor general at Québec City. Governors general spend at least part of each year at the Citadelle as part of their official duties. Since 1920 it has also been home to the Royal 22e Régiment.

49. C. Wiarton

Each February 2, a guy dressed to the nines and standing next to another guy in a white groundhog costume reaches into the town-sponsored den of the famous white woodchuck, Wiarton Willie, pulls him from his snug-as-a-bug-in-a-rug den, foists him high into the air and hopes the pink-eyed little albino can give some indication as to whether he sees his shadow or not.

50. B. Lester B. Pearson

Pearson saw the adoption of the flag by Parliament on December 16, 1964. The Queen gave royal ascent to the adoption of the flag on February 16, 1965. On the stroke of noon that day, the maple leaf flag was hoisted on high and flown on Parliament Hill for the first time.

51. B. February 15

CANADIAN EMBLEMS, HOLIDAYS AND OBSERVANCES

QUESTIONS 52 – 53

52. Match the official flags depicted on the left with the corresponding province on the right.

1.
2.
3.
4.
5.
6.
7.
8.
9.
10.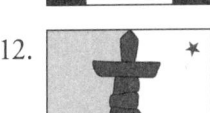
11.
12.
13.

a) Prince Edward Island
b) British Columbia
c) New Brunswick
d) Québec
e) Nunavut
f) Alberta
g) Newfoundland and Labrador
h) Ontario
i) Yukon
j) Manitoba
k) Nova Scotia
l) Northwest Territories
m) Saskatchewan

53. What sunny province has the western red lily as its floral emblem?
   A. British Columbia
   B. Saskatchewan
   C. Ontario

52.

1. b) British Columbia

2. f) Alberta

3. m) Saskatchewan

4. j) Manitoba

5. h) Ontario

6. d) Québec

7. c) New Brunswick

8. k) Nova Scotia

9. a) Prince Edward Island

10. g) Newfoundland and Labrador

11. l) Northwest Territories

12. e) Nunavut
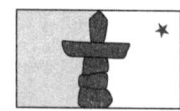

13. i) Yukon

53. B. Saskatchewan

CANADIAN EMBLEMS, HOLIDAYS AND OBSERVANCES

QUESTIONS 54 – 58

54. Which eastern province has the pitcher plant as its floral emblem?
    A. Newfoundland and Labrador
    B. Nova Scotia
    C. Prince Edward Island

55. Which of the following is the highest rank in the Canadian Army or Air Force?
    A. General
    B. Brigadier General
    C. Major General

56. Which of the following is the highest rank in the Canadian Navy?
    A. Admiral
    B. Vice Admiral
    C. Commodore

57. Which province or territory has the fireweed as its floral emblem?
    A. Northwest Territories
    B. Saskatchewan
    C. Yukon

58. What is the name of Canada's official residence for the Leader of the Opposition?
    A. Kingsmere
    B. Rockcliffeway
    C. Stornoway

Answers 54–58

54. A. Newfoundland and Labrador

And why is it called a pitcher plant? Because part of the darned thing can fill with water just like a water pitcher, not because it catches a lot of fly balls.

55. A. General

The officer ranks, from highest to lowest, are general, lieutenant general, major general, brigadier general, colonel, lieutenant colonel, major, captain, lieutenant, second lieutenant, officer cadet.

56. A. Admiral

The officer ranks, from highest to lowest, are admiral, vice admiral, rear admiral, commodore, captain, commander, lieutenant commander, lieutenant, sublieutenant, acting sublieutenant, officer cadet.

57. C. Yukon

Fireweed gets its name because its one of the first plants to grow after a fire.

58. C. Stornoway

The residence was previously occupied by Princess Juliana of the Netherlands during World War II. It was purchased in 1950 by a private group and designated as the official residence of the Leader of the Opposition. It was officially transferred to the Government of Canada in 1970.

CANADIAN EMBLEMS, HOLIDAYS AND OBSERVANCES

Questions 59 – 62

59. Has Canada officially adopted the maple leaf as its floral emblem?
   A. Yes
   B. No

60. Which province or territory has the Pacific dogwood as its floral emblem?
   A. Northwest Territories
   B. Yukon
   C. British Columbia

61. On the first Monday of what month does Alberta observe Heritage Day, New Brunswick observe New Brunswick Day, and other provinces observe a civic holiday?
   A. June
   B. July
   C. August

62. Which territory has the gyrfalcon as its official bird?
   A. Yukon
   B. Northwest Territories
   C. Nunavut

ANSWERS 59 – 62

59. B. No

60. C. British Columbia

61. C. August

The first Monday in August is observed under different names across the country. British Columbia calls it British Columbia Day; Alberta calls it Heritage Day; Saskatchewan calls it Saskatchewan Day; in Nova Scotia and Prince Edward Island it's called Natal Day; in Manitoba, Nunavut and Northwest Territories, it's called a civic holiday; and in Ontario it's either a civic holiday or Simcoe Day. Newfoundland and Labrador, Québec and Yukon don't observe a holiday on that day.

62. B. Northwest Territories

CANADIAN EMBLEMS, HOLIDAYS AND OBSERVANCES

QUESTIONS 63 – 67

63. Who is the commander-in-chief of Canada?
  A. The prime minister
  B. The chief of defence staff
  C. The governor general

64. What is the name of the governor general's official residence?
  A. Stornoway
  B. Rideau Hall
  C. The Residence at Harrington Lake

65. Which province has the common loon as its official bird?
  A. Manitoba
  B. Québec
  C. Ontario

66. What is Canada's official bird?
  A. Canada Goose
  B. Robin
  C. There is no official bird

67. What self-proclaimed "Chicken Capital of Western Canada" holds Chicken Chariot Races as part of its annual carnival in June?
  A. Wynyard, Saskatchewan
  B. Lumsden, Saskatchewan
  C. Regina, Saskatchewan

WHAT IS CANADA?

Answers 63 – 67

63. C. The governor general

64. B. Rideau Hall

The stone villa that forms the main part of the official residence was built by Thomas MacKay in 1838. A stonemason, MacKay also was involved in building the entrance locks of the Rideau Canal and the mills at Rideau Falls. Rideau Hall is named for those landmarks and has been the home of our governor general since Confederation.

65. C. Ontario

School children ages 9–11 chose the common loon as Ontario's official bird. What else can be said except perhaps, "Oops!"

66. C. There is no official bird

67. A. Wynyard, Saskatchewan

There are four lanes per heat in the Chicken Chariot Races, each one divided by a Plexiglas runner. Each chicken pulls one chariot. Chickens are apparently not that bright and they are easily frightened, so if you attach a tiny chariot to them, they run like the dickens. The record for the fastest race is somewhere in the vicinity of 20 seconds over a 15-metre course.

CANADIAN EMBLEMS, HOLIDAYS AND OBSERVANCES

QUESTIONS 68 – 72

68. Which province has the sharp-tailed grouse as its official bird?
A. New Brunswick
B. Saskatchewan
C. Manitoba

69. Who was the first Canadian to be awarded the Victoria Cross?
A. Alexander Mackenzie
B. Alexander Roberts Dunn
C. Lincoln Alexander

70. Which province or territory has the snowy owl as its official bird?
A. Nunavut
B. Québec
C. Yukon

71. Which Canadian and British monarch was succeeded by Elizabeth II?
A. Edward VIII
B. George V
C. George VI

72. What is the two-letter postal abbreviation for Newfoundland and Labrador?
A. NF
B. NL
C. ND

Answers 68 – 72

68. B. Saskatchewan

69. B. Alexander Roberts Dunn

Dunn was awarded the Victoria Cross (VC) for his actions on October 25, 1854, at the Battle of Balaclava during the Crimean War. Dunn's regiment, the British Army's 11th Hussars, joined with the infamous Light Brigade on their disastrous charge that day. Dunn was 21 years old and his VC-winning actions included rescuing a sergeant after cutting down a number of Russian lancers who had attacked from the rear. He also killed another Russian soldier that same day. Dunn was originally born in York (Toronto) in 1833. After Balaclava he went on to become a colonel and commanded the 33rd Regiment of Foot during the 1868 Expedition to Abyssinia. He died during a hunting accident at Senafe under what were called mysterious circumstances. (I have been assured that Dick Cheney wasn't involved though.) His grave is in present-day Eritrea, and copies of his medals are on display at Toronto's Upper Canada College. The original Victoria Cross is apparently in the school's safety deposit box.

70. B. Québec

71. C. George VI

72. A. NF

Questions 73 – 77

73. Which province has the black-capped chickadee as its official bird?
A. Prince Edward Island
B. Nova Scotia
C. New Brunswick

74. What is the English translation of Canada's motto, "A mari usque ad mare"?
A. From mountain to ocean
B. From ship to shore
C. From sea to sea

75. Which province has BC jade as its official gemstone?
A. Alberta
B. British Columbia
C. Saskatchewan

76. What is the name of Canada's official residence for the Speaker of the House of Commons?
A. The Farm at Kingsmere
B. Harrington Lake Residence
C. The Citadelle

77. Which western province has the Stellar's jay as its official bird?
A. British Columbia
B. Saskatchewan
C. Alberta

Answers 73 – 77

73. C. New Brunswick

74. C. From sea to sea

75. B. British Columbia
No trick question here!

76. A. The Farm at Kingsmere
It is located on the Mackenzie King Estate in Gatineau Park and was bequeathed to the people of Canada by William Lyon Mackenzie King after his death in 1950.

77. A. British Columbia

CANADIAN EMBLEMS, HOLIDAYS AND OBSERVANCES

Questions 78 – 81

78. In the Canadian entertainment industry, what do the letters ACTRA stand for?
   A. Association of Craft, Technical and Radio Artists
   B. Assembly of Creative, Technical and Retired Actors
   C. Association of Canadian Television and Radio Artists

79. What Canadian government organization has the abbreviation CSA?
   A. Canadian Spy Agency
   B. Canadian Space Agency
   C. Canadian Surveillance and Intelligence Agency

80. In British Columbia, what fair is abbreviated PNE?
   A. Penticton Native Exhibition
   B. Pacific National Exhibition
   C. Pacific Nuclear Exhibition

81. What statutory holiday is observed in Canada in May?
   A. St. Jean Baptiste Day
   B. Veterans Day
   C. Victoria Day

ANSWERS 78–81

78. C. Association of Canadian Television and Radio Artists

79. B. Canadian Space Agency

It's sort of our equivalent of NASA. The CSA was established in 1989, and the agency has five functions: Space Programs, Space Technologies, Space Science, Canadian Astronaut Office and Space Operations.

80. B. Pacific National Exhibition

81. C. Victoria Day

Questions 82–86

82. On the Canadian coat of arms, what country is represented by the harp?

A. Ireland
B. England
C. France

83. What Canadian-born hero was the first black man awarded the Victoria Cross?

A. William Hall
B. Montieth Hall
C. Hal Wallace

84. What two animals are depicted on the Canadian coat of arms?

A. Dragon and mule
B. Lion and leopard
C. Lion and unicorn

85. What is the two-letter postal abbreviation for Nunavut?

A. NV
B. NT
C. NU

86. In 1965, who proposed the basic design of the Canadian flag?

A. Bertha Wilson
B. John Diefenbaker
C. George F.G. Stanley

Answers 82–86

82. A. Ireland

83. A. William Hall

Hall was not only the first black man to receive the Victoria Cross (VC), but he was also the first Nova Scotian to receive it and only the third Canadian recipient. Hall was travelling to China on HMS *Shannon* when the Indian Mutiny broke out in May 1857. The ship was redirected to Calcutta and was eventually towed up the Ganges to Allahabad. Hall won his VC during the attack on the Shah Nujeff mosque in Lucknow. Hall and a number of other men withstood a withering barrage of musket balls and grenades. In the end though, only he and Lieutenant Thomas Young survived the barrage. Hall eventually rose to the rank of Quartermaster Petty Officer on HMS *Peterel*. He retired in 1876 and died at Avonport, Nova Scotia, in August 1904. Despite his distinguished service, Hall was buried in an unmarked grave without military honours. In 1945 his remains were moved to Hantsport Baptist Church and a monument was erected. His medals were displayed at Expo '67 and are now at the Nova Scotia Museum.

84. C. Lion and unicorn

85. C. NU

86. C. George F.G. Stanley

In addition to designing the flag, Stanley, born in Calgary in 1907, became the lieutenant-governor of New Brunswick in 1982.

CANADIAN EMBLEMS, HOLIDAYS AND OBSERVANCES

Questions 87 – 91

87. What is the capital city of Yukon?
   A. Yellowknife
   B. Moose Jaw
   C. Whitehorse

88. What did Dominion Day become known as in 1982?
   A. Victoria Day
   B. Canada Day
   C. Confederation Day

89. Which province has the great grey owl as its official bird?
   A. Manitoba
   B. Ontario
   C. Saskatchewan

90. In Canada, what is the highest medal for bravery?
   A. Cross de Lis
   B. Cross of Valour
   C. Harbour Cross

91. Our motto, "From sea to sea," could not really apply to Canada until 1871, when what province joined Confederation?
   A. British Columbia
   B. Newfoundland
   C. Prince Edward Island

ANSWERS 87–91

87. C. Whitehorse

88. B. Canada Day

89. A. Manitoba

90. B. Cross of Valour

The Cross of Valour was initiated by the Queen in 1972 and is presented by the governor general. It is awarded only for "acts of conspicuous courage in circumstances of extreme peril." To date, the Cross of Valour has only been awarded 19 times. Recipients of the Cross of Valour may use the initials "C.V." after their name.

91. A. British Columbia

Canadian Emblems, Holidays and Observances

92. The official motto of what province is "Loyal she began, Loyal she remains"?
   A. Nova Scotia
   B. Québec
   C. Ontario

93. In Canada, what holiday is observed on the first Monday in September?
   A. Thanksgiving
   B. Labour Day
   C. Remembrance Day

94. What is the name of the official summer residence of Canada's prime minister and has been the site of many a constitutional chat?
   A. La Mec
   B. Harrington Lake Residence
   C. Lake Memphremagog Residence

95. Canada's motto, "A mari usque ad mare," is taken from what book in the King James version of the Bible?
   A. Proverbs
   B. Psalms
   C. Revelation

Answers 92–95

92. C. Ontario

93. B. Labour Day

94. B. Harrington Lake Residence

The residence comprises 13 acres of grounds and one main building that contains 16 rooms. There are also eight outbuildings. It sits on the edge of Lac Mousseau in Gatineau Park and was originally built by a lumber baron named Colonel Cameron Macpherson Edwards. It became an almost infamous meeting place for constitutional talks during Brian Mulroney's administration. No word, though, on whether envelopes of money ever arrived there.

95. B. Psalms

QUESTIONS 96 – 100

96. What meat pie is made with ground pork and served at Christmas in many French Canadian homes?
A. Tortellini
B. Bacalhau
C. Tortière

97. On what day do Canadians observe Remembrance Day?
A. November 11
B. May 24
C. February 15

98. In what province is an annual festival dedicated to peat moss celebrated in a town named Lamèque?
A. Québec
B. New Brunswick
C. Manitoba

99. What is the two-letter postal abbreviation for Prince Edward Island?
A. PE
B. PI
C. EI

100. Which "royal" museum is located in Midland Provincial Park?
A. Royal Ontario Museum
B. Royal British Columbia Museum
C. Royal Tyrrell Museum

ANSWERS 96 – 100

96. C. Tortière

97. A. November 11

98. B. New Brunswick

The Peat Moss Festival is actually officially called "Festival Provincial de la Tourbe," and it rears its mossy head each July. It's a week-long celebration of all things peaty, and it has been going on for some 36 years.

99. A. PE

100. C. Royal Tyrrell Museum

The museum is located near Drumheller, Alberta, in Midland Provincial Park. As most Canadians know, it is a paleontology museum and research facility named for Joseph Burr Tyrrell. It opened in 1985 and was given "royal" status in 1990.

THE PRE-CONFEDERATION HISTORY OF CANADA

Our pre-Confederation history—from the first humans to the official founding of our Dominion—is actually a much longer time than our post-Confederation history. It's full of battles, struggles and one or two odd and almost miraculous figures, heroes and dunces. So take your time, take your chances and test your skill at the wild and weary, calm and chaotic and mostly chronologically ordered questions in this "Canada before there was a Canada" chapter of historical proportions.

101. The first humans arrived in what is now Canada between…
   A. 10,000 and 50,000 years ago
   B. 75,000 and 125,000 years ago
   C. 150,000 and 300,000 years ago

102. The first humans arrived in the Americas by a land bridge connecting…
   A. Europe to North America
   B. Africa to South America
   C. Asia to North America

103. When did the first Europeans reach North America?
   A. 8th century
   B. 10th century
   C. 13th century

WHAT IS CANADA?

ANSWERS 100 – 103

101. A. 10,000 and 50,000 years ago

Scientists estimate that the first humans arrived in North America between 10,000 and 50,000 years ago. The date generally accepted is 12,000 years ago, but the date is still under dispute. Scientific and archaeological knowledge and "fact" are ever-evolving, so the dates could eventually be pushed back. The arrival of these peoples took place during the Pleistocene epoch.

102. C. Asia to North America

The land bridge actually connected what is now Siberia with what is now Alaska. And although it is generally called a "land bridge," it was really just the floor of the ocean, where the Bering Strait is today, which was exposed during the last Ice Age (70,000–11,000). Glaciers sucked up vast amounts of ocean water during the Ice Age and exposed the continental shelves, thus providing a convenient and pretty much ice-free route to travel to vast new lands. Why humans came to the Americas is still a matter of theory and speculation.

103. B. 10th century

QUESTIONS 104–107

104. Who do scholars generally accept as being the first European to reach the North American mainland?
   A. Bjarni Herjolfsson
   B. Eric the Red
   C. John Cabot

105. Where was the first authentic Norse site found in North America?
   A. Labrador
   B. St. John's
   C. L'Anse aux Meadows

106. What did the Vikings call Newfoundland?
   A. Markland
   B. Helluland
   C. Vinland

107. What religious order played an important part in French colonization of New France and was founded in 1534 by Ignatius Loyala?
   A. Bennetons
   B. Jesuits
   C. Franciscans

104. A. Bjarni Herjolfsson

Around about 985, a Norse merchant and trader named Bjarni Herjolfsson got lost on his way to Greenland in stormy seas. He saw a number of new lands that he described as variously wooded, hilly and mountainous. The lands he sighted were most likely Newfoundland, Labrador and Baffin Island, though some scholars have suggested he may have sailed as far south as the modern-day U.S. state of Maine.

105. C. L'Anse aux Meadows

L'Anse aux Meadows was discovered on the northern tip of Newfoundland by Norwegians Helge Ingstad and his wife Anne Stine Ingstad in 1960. Now a UNESCO World Heritage Site, L'Anse aux Meadows consists of the remains of three buildings that each contain living areas and workshops. Carpentry and iron working took place here as well as iron smelting.

106. C. Vinland

Vinland was so named by Lief Erikson because he found wild grapes growing around tall trees. Markland, or Land of Forests, is most probably a region near Hamilton Inlet in Labrador. Helluland, or Land of Stone Slabs, was characterized by mountains, rock and glaciers. It is most likely an area ranging from Baffin Island to the Torngat Mountains (Cape Chidley, Labrador).

107. B. Jesuits

The Jesuits were also known as the Society of Jesus, or Company of Jesus. As part of their missionary work, the Jesuits came to New France to convert Native people to Catholicism. After the British conquest of New France, the Jesuits were suppressed.

Questions 108–111

108. On June 24, 1497, what Italian navigator landed on the Atlantic coast of North America and claimed it for England?

A. John Cabot
B. Jacques Cartier
C. Giovanni da Verrazzano

109. What explorer landed at Gaspé in 1534 and was the first European to discover the St. Lawrence River?

A. Jacques Cartier
B. Giovanni da Verrazzano
C. Gaspar Corte-Real

110. Who was the first European to discover Prince Edward Island?

A. Jacques Cartier
B. Giovanni da Verrazzano
C. Gaspar Corte-Real

111. In 1500, what explorer claimed North America for Portugal while on a voyage that reached Greenland and Newfoundland?

A. Giovanni da Verrazzano
B. Gaspar Corte-Real
C. Pedro Barcelos

108. A. John Cabot

John Cabot, or Giovanni Caboto (his original Italian name), was probably born in Gaeta near Naples in Italy (according to Heritage Canada). Under a grant from England's King Henry VII, Cabot landed either at Cape Bonavista, Newfoundland, or at Cape Breton Island on June 24, 1497.

109. A. Jacques Cartier

Born in St. Malo, France, Cartier led three voyages to the St. Lawrence region: 1534, 1535–36 and 1541–42. He raised a cross on the shores of the Baie de Gaspé after meeting a group of Iroquois.

110. A. Jacques Cartier

He discovered Prince Edward Island for France on June 29, 1534.

111. B. Gaspar Corte-Real

Portuguese claims to the North Atlantic date from the voyage of Gaspar Corte-Real in 1500. He was born in the Azores. His initial voyage saw him reach Greenland and then head south to Newfoundland. On a second voyage in 1501 he explored the Labrador coast and may have gotten as far as Baffin Island. Two of the vessels from that voyage returned to Portugal; however, Gaspar Corte-Real's ship did not. He was never heard from again, and neither were his two brothers, who undertook separate voyages to find him and also suffered the same fate: they were never heard from again. The Portuguese may have actually been the earliest European explorers to see what is now Canada. Their discoveries and claims on Canada may date as far back as 1542 with Diogo de Tieve.

Questions 112–116

112. Giovanni Caboto reached North America for the first time with 18 men aboard what ship?

A. *Endeavour*
B. *Matthew*
C. *Nonsuch*

113. Who was the first Iroquois chief that Jacques Cartier encountered?

A. Stadacona
B. Hochelaga
C. Donnacona

114. Which explorer is called the "Father of New France"?

A. Jacques Cartier
B. John Cabot
C. Samuel de Champlain

115. In 1535, Jacques Cartier reached what Iroquois village located at the site of present-day Montréal?

A. Ville Marie
B. Hochelaga
C. Stadacona

116. In 1608, where did Samuel de Champlain found France's first permanent colony in New France?

A. Québec
B. Ville Marie
C. Detroit

Answers 112–116

112. B. *Matthew*

113. C. Donnacona

Donnacona was the chief of the Iroquois at the village of Stadacona. On Cartier's second voyage to New France in 1535–36, Donnacona was seized and taken back to France where he was presented to King Francis I. Donnacona died in France in 1539.

114. C. Samuel de Champlain

115. B. Hochelaga

Cartier arrived in 1535 at Hochelaga, a village inhabited by about 1500 Iroquois. The French climbed Mount Royal, and offended the Iroquois by not participating in a feast prepared in their honour and then leaving rather abruptly. When the French returned in 1603, the Hochelagans had vanished.

116. A. Québec

117. What Catholic utopian colony was founded by Paul de Chomeday de Maisonneuve on May 17, 1642?
   A. Detroit
   B. Port Royal
   C. Ville Marie

118. What First Nations people were destroyed and dispersed by Iroquois raids in 1649?
   A. Blackfoot
   B. Huron
   C. Cree

119. The first official census of Canada and the Great Fire of London both happened in what year?
   A. 1555
   B. 1635
   C. 1666

120. Who originally commissioned the practice of scalping?
   A. The British
   B. Huron
   C. The French

121. In 1665, who became the first Intendant of New France?
   A. Jean Talon
   B. Gilles Hocquart
   C. François Bigot

117. C. Ville Marie

Ville Marie was founded on the Île de Montréal by the Societe Notre-Dame de Montréal under Governor Paul de Chomeday de Maissonneuve with the idea of bringing Christianity to the Native people.

118. B. Huron

The Huron were a confederacy of five Iroquoian-speaking tribes. They called themselves the Ouendat (Wendat). Before 1600 the Huron numbered more than 20,000, but by 1640 their numbers were reduced to fewer than 10,000, mostly by disease. The Iroquois defeated the Huron in 1649. Some Huron joined the Iroquois and others fled west.

119. C. 1666

120. A. The British

They paid for the scalps of enemy First Nations people.

121. A. Jean Talon

King Louis XIV created the Office of Intendant in 1663. The Intendant was second in rank to the governor and controlled the civil administration of the colony. Jean Talon, as the first Intendant, was in charge of encouraging settlement in the colony and making it thrive.

Questions 122–125

122. In 1702, what war broke out between France and England that led to the eventual capture of Port Royal?

A. War of the Polish Succession
B. War of the Austrian Succession
C. Queen Anne's War

123. The 1713 Treaty of Utrecht confirmed British control over Newfoundland, Acadia and what body of water?

A. Hudson Bay
B. Lake Huron
C. Lake Superior

124. What French explorer searched for a route from Lake Superior to the Prairies?

A. Jolliet
B. Radisson
C. La Vérendrye

125. In 1749, Edward Cornwallis arrived in Chebucto Harbour and founded which Canadian city?

A. St. John
B. St. John's
C. Halifax

122. C. Queen Anne's War

This was the North American counterpart to Europe's War of the Spanish Succession. The term "Queen Anne's War" is mostly used in the United States.

123. A. Hudson Bay

124. C. La Vérendrye

Pierre Gaultier de Varennes et de La Vérendrye was born at Trois Rivières in 1685. A man characterized by wanderlust, La Vérendrye succeeded his brother as commandant of fur-trading posts along Lake Superior. From that moment in 1728 and onward, he searched for a route to the western sea. He incrementally moved west to Lake Winnipeg and then to Fort La Reine (Portage La Prairie). He and his sons were involved in a number of expeditions that explored the Missouri River and the Saskatchewan River.

125. C. Halifax

Halifax replaced Annapolis Royal as the capital of Nova Scotia. Its founding gave the British a strong foothold in Nova Scotia and an excellent counterpart to Louisbourg.

THE PRE-CONFEDERATION HISTORY OF CANADA

QUESTIONS 126 – 129

126. Who did the British expel from Nova Scotia in 1755 because they refused to pledge an oath of allegiance to Britain?
   A. Acadians
   B. Micmacs
   C. Gypsies

127. Which war took place from 1756 to 1763 and is considered the first global war?
   A. War of the Austrian Succession
   B. War of the Roses
   C. Seven Years' War

128. On what plains was the September 13, 1759 battle of Québec decided in favour of the British?
   A. Elesian Fields
   B. Plains of Abraham
   C. Plains of Joshua

129. In 1763, who led an alliance of western First Nations tribes against the British and managed to capture a number of posts including Detroit and Michilimackinac?
   A. Pontiac
   B. Geronimo
   C. Joseph Brant

Answers 126–129

126. A. Acadians

Most of the Acadian population of Nova Scotia were rounded up and forcibly sent back to France or to the lower British colonies. Some Acadians fled deeper into Nova Scotia or into New France. Many exiled Acadians eventually settled in Louisiana, which was transferred by France to Spain before the end of the French and Indian Wars.

127. C. Seven Years' War

The North American theatre of the war actually lasted for nine years.

128. B. Plains of Abraham

They are sometimes referred to as the "heights of Abraham," and they are located outside the western edge of the old walled city. They are not biblically named as some people think, but were instead named for Abraham Martin, a ship's pilot who once owned the land. Check the Military History chapter for more fun-filled and battle-weary questions on this and other battles of the Seven Years' War.

129. A. Pontiac

A series of peace treaties were signed with the British in 1765. As Pontiac signed onto the treaties, he made it clear that the First Nations were not surrendering themselves or their lands. Nevertheless, many First Nations remained hostile to the British and turned against Pontiac. He was even expelled from his own village and forced to wander the rest of his life, which ended when he was assassinated in 1769.

Questions 130–133

130. What 1774 legislation provided for British criminal law but restored French civil law and religious freedom for Roman Catholic colonists?

   A. Québec Act
   B. Quartering Act
   C. Administration of Justice Act

131. Who did rebel Americans try unsuccessfully to get to join their war of independence against Britain?

   A. French Québecers
   B. Inuit
   C. Huron

132. What action did the American rebels take against Québec in 1775?

   A. Ignored them
   B. Wooed them with Bavarian chocolate and nylons
   C. Attacked them with a military force

133. What term was used to describe American colonials who remained loyal to Britain?

   A. Patriots
   B. Rebels
   C. Loyalists

130. A. Québec Act

The Québec Act along with the "Intolerable Acts," which included the Quartering Act, Administration of Justice Act, Boston Port Bill, and the Massachusetts Government Act, gave American colonists justification for their revolution. The Québec Act, though not part of the Intolerable Acts, did give Americans a rallying cry for justice, raising the spectre of papal interference since Québecers were granted religious freedom and they were Catholic, while the American colonies were mainly Protestant.

131. A. French Québecers

Québecers wanted no part of the American cause since they had already been guaranteed religious freedoms and Civil Law thanks to the Québec Act, and probably also because the American colonies were rabidly Protestant and no guarantee of Québec's cultural freedoms was forthcoming.

132. C. Attacked them with a military force

The Americans captured Montréal in 1775 and blockaded Québec City until May 1776.

133. C. Loyalists

"Rebels" and "patriots" were terms used to describe the American colonials who took up arms against Britain or supported American independence from Britain.

Questions 134–137

134. The arrival of Loyalists from the American colonies in Nova Scotia and Québec eventually resulted in the formation of what new colonies?
   A. British Columbia and Alberta
   B. Manitoba and Ontario
   C. Upper Canada and New Brunswick

135. What 1791 legislation divided Québec into Upper and Lower Canada?
   A. Treaty of Paris
   B. Constitutional Act
   C. LC-UC Act

136. Who arrived at Nootka Sound in 1792, undertook futile negotiations over territory with the Spanish and then spent the rest of that summer and the summers of 1793 and 1794 exploring Puget Sound and the mainland coast of what would eventually become British Columbia?
   A. Alexander Mackenzie
   B. Captain James Cook
   C. George Vancouver

137. Who arrived at Bella Coola in 1793, marking the completion of the first overland journey across North America?
   A. Alexander Mackenzie
   B. Captain James Cook
   C. George Vancouver

Answers 134–137

134. C. Upper Canada and New Brunswick

135. B. Constitutional Act

136. C. George Vancouver

Vancouver was a naval officer who had previously accompanied James Cook on his South Seas and Northwest Coast voyages. After the Spanish seized Nootka Sound, Vancouver was sent to retrieve the properties. It didn't happen quite as planned, and the territorial negotiations were sent back to London and Madrid. Vancouver stayed on and explored much of British Columbia over three summers, spending winters in Hawaii. Not a bad gig if you can get it.

137. A. Alexander Mackenzie

Although Mackenzie and his party reached the Pacific via the Bella Coola River, his achievement failed to provide a viable route for fur traders.

Questions 138–141

138. In 1805, who established the first trading post at Fort McLeod on Trout Lake in what is now British Columbia?

A. James McGill
B. Simon Fraser
C. Lord Selkirk

139. Which fur trader bequeathed much of his estate to the founding of a university that bears his name?

A. James McGill
B. Simon Fraser
C. Alexander Mackenzie

140. Alexander Mackenzie and Simon Fraser were employed by what rival to the Hudson's Bay Company?

A. Sears
B. East India Company
C. North West Company

141. In 1811, who established a colony at Red River thanks to a grant of land from the Hudson's Bay Company?

A. James McGill
B. Simon Fraser
C. Lord Selkirk

138. B. Simon Fraser

139. A. James McGill

McGill died in 1813 and was apparently the richest person in Montréal at that time. Simon Fraser University in Burnaby, BC, was not established until 1965, and it wasn't bequeathed any money by its namesake.

140. C. North West Company

141. C. Lord Selkirk

The Hudson's Bay Company granted Selkirk lands amounting to 185,000 square kilometres specifically to set up a colony. It was the first European colony in the North-West, and despite trials and tribulations, it did thrive and was the forerunner to the province of Manitoba.

Questions 142–145

142. What military commander died at Queenston Heights on October 12, 1812, and is referred to as the "Saviour of Upper Canada"?
   A. Francis Gore
   B. Sir Isaac Brock
   C. John Graves Simcoe

143. In 1839, what waterway opened connecting Lake Erie with Lake Ontario?
   A. Erie Canal
   B. Rideau Canal
   C. Welland Canal

144. What disease spread as an epidemic in 1832 and prompted government officials to open a quarantine station at Grosse Île near Québec City?
   A. Cholera
   B. Small pox
   C. Tuberculosis

145. What happened in 1837 that sent Lord Durham to the Canadas to investigate and write a report?
   A. Influenza epidemic
   B. Recession
   C. Rebellion

142. B. Sir Isaac Brock

He was killed by a sharpshooter's bullet while leading his men and turning back an invasion by New York militia.

143. C. Welland Canal

The canal opened the way west, but also provided economic advantages for transportation and shipping that helped rival the Erie Canal in the U.S.

144. A. Cholera

All ships stopped at the quarantine stations on Grosse Île near Québec City during the cholera epidemic. The quarantine did little good in combating the epidemic that killed nearly 10 percent of the Québec population.

145. C. Rebellion

Upper and Lower Canada each faced rebellion or insurrection depending on which side of the fence your loyalties leaned. The rebellions were not terribly successful. There were some deaths, some fires and even shots fired. Eventually there were also executions, fleeing rebel leaders and ultimately Lord Durham's report, which united the two Canadas and indirectly led to responsible government.

146. What 19th-century clandestine organization helped slaves flee the U.S. for British North America?

   A. Unterseeboot
   B. Overland Express
   C. Underground Railroad

147. On what river was there a gold rush in 1858 that saw 30,000 fortune hunters head to what is now British Columbia?

   A. Columbia River
   B. Klondike River
   C. Fraser River

148. In 1850, one of the great missions of history began to search for what arctic explorer who captained HMS *Erebus*?

   A. Henry Stanley
   B. Ernest Shackleton
   C. Sir John Franklin

149. What treaty was signed in 1854 between the U.S. and the colony of Canada and set in motion the reduction of customs duties?

   A. Reciprocity Treaty
   B. Maastrich Treaty
   C. NAFTA

ANSWERS 146 – 149

146. C. Underground Railroad

The Underground Railroad was an informal network of people, safe houses and safe stopping points that helped fugitive slaves flee slave states and safely pass to free states or to Canada. Some 25,000 or more fugitive slaves actually reached Canada.

147. C. Fraser River

148. C. Sir John Franklin

In 1845, Franklin took HMS *Erebus* and *Terror* into the Arctic to prove there was a Northwest Passage. In fact, he did prove it, but since he and all of those with him perished, it took nine more years for the truth to come out. Franklin owes much of his fame to the 12-year search for him and his crew.

149. A. Reciprocity Treaty

It produced much trade between Canada and the U.S. and was popular in Canada, though the U.S. did not renew it in 1866.

QUESTIONS 150 – 154

150. What 1846 treaty set the border between the U.S. and British North America at 49° north latitude?
   A. Oregon Treaty
   B. Alaska Boundary Treaty
   C. King George Treaty Act

151. Who is so far the only Canadian-born British prime minister?
   A. David Lloyd George
   B. Benjamin Disraeli
   C. Andrew Bonar Law

152. In what Prince Edward Island city was the first conference held that led to Canada's Confederation?
   A. Charlottetown
   B. Georgetown
   C. Tignish

153. What part of Canada pushed for Confederation to establish its cultural identity?
   A. Canada West
   B. Canada East
   C. New Brunswick

154. What 1866 Irish raids helped convince New Brunswick to join Confederation?
   A. Gapp Raids
   B. Nimby Raids
   C. Fenian Raids

150. A. Oregon Treaty

The treaty left Vancouver Island in British hands and made for an equitable division of the West.

151. C. Andrew Bonar Law

In addition to being the only Canadian-born British prime minister, Andrew Bonar Law is also, so far, the only colonial British prime minister. Born in 1858 in New Brunswick, he served in governments of Herbert Asquith and Lloyd George. He signed the Treaty of Versailles in 1919 on behalf of Great Britain and later forced Lloyd George's resignation. In 1922 Andrew Bonar Law became British Conservative leader and prime minister, an office he held for just seven months. He was forced to retire because of ill health and died within a year, on October 30, 1923.

152. A. Charlottetown

The first conference was held in 1864.

153. B. Canada East

154. C. Fenian Raids

The Fenians were a group of Irish Americans intent on forcing the independence of Ireland on Britain. When no uprising happened in Ireland itself, the American Fenians launched a raid into New Brunswick. The raid fell apart almost as soon as it began. The only lasting result was that it turned opinion in much of the Maritimes for Confederation. The Fenians continued to cause problems in Canada and the U.S. and probably up to the time of the Easter 1916 uprising in Dublin, Ireland.

THE EDUCATION OF A CANADIAN, ALONG WITH UNIQUELY CANADIAN WORDS

Taking a look at the subject of education from two different ends may provide a unique look inside the culture of a people. So in this chapter of Q&A, higher education plays a pivotal role, but right alongside it go a great many everyday words and phrases that just about everyone in Canada uses. Canada is a vast and bleak (I write this in the dead of winter) place, but always a beautiful and surprising land full of uniquely odd people and their way of speechifying, eh?

155. At Tim Hortons, what is the most common way to order coffee with two creams and two sugars?

A. Two-two
B. Cream-sug
C. Double-double

156. What term is used in sports, and most often in hockey, to describe a quick move that fakes out an opponent?

A. Quit
B. Deke
C. Bawk

155. C. Double-double

The phrase may or may not have originated with Tim Hortons, though for sure, it is understood in each and every one of the franchises.

156. B. Deke

QUESTIONS 157 – 160

157. Which of the following terms is the traditional way that Canadians refer to a case of beer…with 24 bottles?
   A. Poverty pack
   B. Two-four
   C. Twenty-fourer

158. Which Alberta university specializes in courses and programs delivered through distance education, including the Internet?
   A. Athabasca University
   B. University of Calgary
   C. University of Lethbridge

159. Which of the following words is the same thing as a napkin?
   A. Serviette
   B. Soup spoon
   C. Waitress

160. Which term was popularized by Bob and Doug McKenzie of SCTV fame and means "Get lost" or "Screw off"?
   A. Hoser
   B. Hightail it
   C. Take off

WHAT IS CANADA?

ANSWERS 157 – 160

157. B. Two-four
It can be pronounced "two-four" or "two-fur."

158. A. Athabasca University
Established in 1970, the university currently serves about 30,000 students per year.

159. A. Serviette

160. C. Take off
The term was also popularized by the film *Strange Brew*, but Canadians don't use this expression…at least no Canadians that I know.

QUESTIONS 161–164

161. Which of the following is a short form that means Canadian Content?

A. Can Club
B. Can-Con
C. B-A-D

162. Which of the following is the equivalent of a 26-ounce bottle of alcohol?

A. Twenty-sixer
B. Bigun
C. Happy flask

163. What university is named after the first bishop of Québec?

A. Concordia University
B. McGill University
C. Laval University

164. What prepared food consists of French fries topped with cheese curd and then smothered in gravy?

A. Poutine
B. Poohteen
C. Gawk

Answers 161–164

161. B. Can-Con
Canadian Content refers to a percentage of content (songs, TV programs, films) that must be aired by Canadian broadcasters on radio and television.

162. A. Twenty-sixer

163. C. Laval University
François Montmorency de Laval was in fact the first Bishop of Canada, appointed in 1658. He died in Québec in 1708. The main campus of the university is located, not surprisingly, in Québec City.

164. A. Poutine
It's a gooey mess that originated in Québec.

THE EDUCATION OF A CANADIAN,
ALONG WITH UNIQUELY CANADIAN WORDS

QUESTIONS 165 – 168

165. Which term describes an extremely easy course at a college or university?

A. College course
B. Bird course
C. Hawk course

166. If Americans call it a "restroom," what do Canadians call it?

A. Bedroom
B. Sitting room
C. Washroom

167. In which city would you find the University of Saskatchewan?

A. Regina
B. Saskatoon
C. Moose Jaw

168. What three-letter abbreviation is the Canadian equivalent of the American Social Security Number?

A. SSN
B. ISB
C. SIN

165. B. Bird course

Presumably it is called this because even a bird could do well in it.

166. C. Washroom

We also call it the Men's Room or Ladies Room.

167. B. Saskatoon

168. C. SIN

The Social Insurance Number (SIN) has nine digits, just like the Social Security Number (SSN), but the SIN is written like this: 123 456 789, whereas the SSN is written like this: 123 45 6789.

Questions 169–173

169. In the Inuit language, Inuktitut, what does "Nunavut" mean?

A. Our land
B. Crop inhibitor
C. Vinland

170. Which of the following was once a very potent, almost gasoline-tasting type of rum that is produced in Newfoundland?

A. Screech
B. Smirnoff
C. Ayesdebye

171. Which of the following is a colloquial way of referring to Sault Ste. Marie, Ontario?

A. Mother Mary
B. The Soo
C. The Rock

172. In the military, what does "DEW" stand for?

A. Distant Early Warship
B. Dismal Early Warfare
C. Distant Early Warning

173. Which of the following universities is located in Newfoundland?

A. St. Francis Xavier University
B. Brock University
C. Memorial University

169. A. Our land

170. A. Screech

171. B. The Soo

172. C. Distant Early Warning
The DEW Line began on February 15, 1954, and is a series of radar sites built in the Arctic to give early warning in case of an over-the-Pole invasion of North America. The construction of the DEW Line was authorized by President Eisenhower. The DEW Line was upgraded and became the North Warning System (NWS) in the 1980s.

173. C. Memorial University
The main campus of Memorial University of Newfoundland is in St. John's, Newfoundland. Brock University is in St. Catharines, Ontario, and St. Francis Xavier is in Antigonish, Nova Scotia.

THE EDUCATION OF A CANADIAN,
ALONG WITH UNIQUELY CANADIAN WORDS

QUESTIONS 174–177

174. What three-letter word is how Canadians refer to carbonated beverages?

A. Sod
B. Pop
C. Car

175. Which of the following is an accepted slang term meaning "Canadian," as well as a term used to describe a member of the NHL team based in Vancouver?

A. Canuck
B. Chinook
C. Lotus flower

176. What sad term denotes a six-pack of beer?

A. Depression pack
B. Poverty pack
C. Morose mickey

177. What is the common name for the one-dollar coin in Canada?

A. Quid
B. Moonie
C. Loonie

WHAT IS CANADA?

ANSWERS 174 – 177

174. B. Pop

It is similar to the way that many Americans call "soda pop," soda. We also refer to pop with their name brands: Coke, Pepsi, Ginger Ale and so on.

175. A. Canuck

176. B. Poverty pack

It is so designated because only the poverty stricken would buy beer in such a small quantity.

177. C. Loonie

It replaced the paper one-dollar bill in the late 1980s. It has the Queen's profile on one side and a loon on the other side and that's why it's called loonie.

Questions 178 – 181

178. What word describes any number of Canadians who reside in the southern United States during the winter months and especially in Florida or Arizona?

A. Snowbird
B. Snow-wus
C. Smartie

179. The First Nations University of Canada is located in which province?

A. Manitoba
B. British Columbia
C. Saskatchewan

180. Which of the following foods is a very tasty cross between ham and bacon that is finished off by being rolled in cornmeal?

A. Poutine
B. Beaver tail
C. Peameal bacon

181. Which of the following words means a warm dry wind that swoops down the eastern slopes of the Rockies and can cause temperatures to rise by 20°C?

A. Coho
B. Alberta clipper
C. Chinook

178. A. Snowbird

It most often refers to senior citizens. The word is also the title of a schmaltzy song by famous Canadian singer Anne Murray.

179. C. Saskatchewan

It is specifically located in Regina where it was founded in 1976 as Saskatchewan Indian Federated College. It was renamed in 2003 and is Canada's only First Nations owned and operated post-secondary institution.

180. C. Peameal bacon

Boneless pork loin was originally cured in pickle brine and then rolled in ground yellow peas. Cornmeal has replaced the peas in modern incarnations, but the name remains the same.

181. C. Chinook

It's also a type of salmon.

182. Which word means a 13-ounce bottle of liquor that can conveniently fit into a pocket?
    A. Mickey
    B. Minnie
    C. Sally

183. Which of the following terms describes a person living in the province of Québec whose native language is other than English or French?
    A. Anglophone
    B. Francophone
    C. Allophone

184. Which of the following two-word phrases means troublemaker?
    A. Bon temp
    B. Clara Bow
    C. Sh** disturber

185. What colourful word is used by Bob and Doug McKenzie on SCTV and in their film *Strange Brew* and means "being taken advantage of"?
    A. Clingy
    B. Hosed
    C. Shnockered

WHAT IS CANADA?

Answers 182–185

182. A. Mickey

183. C. Allophone

184. C. Sh** disturber
It also means practical joker or instigator of any trouble for which things might be better left alone.

185. B. Hosed

QUESTIONS 186 – 189

186. Which of the following is a non-secret, non-paramilitary organization that recruits girls and indoctrinates them with positive values and skills for life, such as being self-sufficient and building campfires?
   A. Boy Scouts
   B. Girl Guides
   C. Olympic Women's Hockey Team

187. What ubiquitous boxed macaroni and cheese meal is also interchangeable with its name brand in Canada?
   A. Poutine
   B. Timbits
   C. Kraft Dinner

188. What is the name of the university in Hamilton, Ontario, whose athletic teams go by the name Marauders?
   A. McMaster University
   B. Wilfrid Laurier University
   C. York University

189. Which of the following words describes a machine from which Canadians retrieve money?
   A. ABM
   B. ATM
   C. Instant Teller

ANSWERS 186 – 189

186. B. Girl Guides

The equivalent of America's "Girl Scouts," the Girl Guides has also been known to raise girls' self-esteem while they live, grow, learn and contribute to their communities.

187. C. Kraft Dinner

The box is navy blue with yellow lettering, and the box dinner includes dry macaroni and a single packet of dried cheese that has a distinctive day-glow orange-yellow colouring. In the United States it is simply sold as Kraft Macaroni and Cheese. How boring! To make Kraft Dinner, you boil the macaroni, add milk and butter and then stir in the powdered cheese. Some Canadians add sliced wieners to the Kraft Dinner to make it more…hearty? Macaroni and cheese not made from the boxed mixture is not referred to as Kraft Dinner. It is simply called macaroni and cheese.

188. A. McMaster University

189. A, B and C

All three are correct.

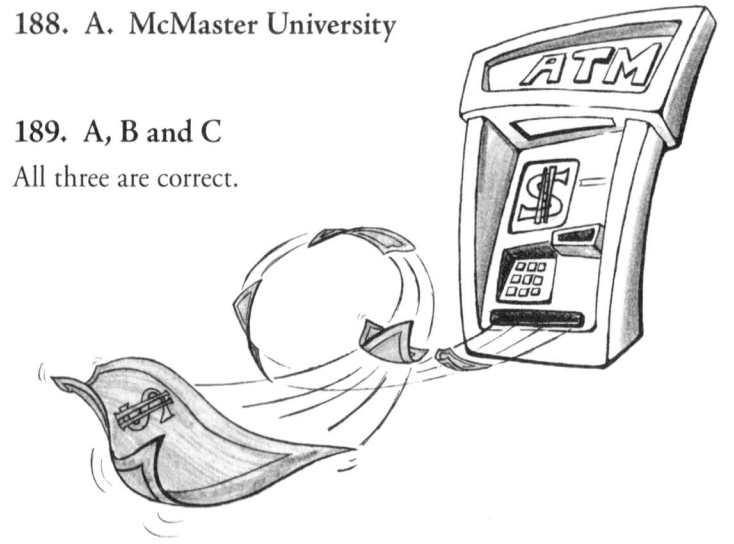

190. In Ontario, what are the government-run liquor stores called?

A. Brewer's Retail
B. LCBO
C. Loo

191. What colloquial term refers to Québec's Office de la Langue Française?

A. Office of Official Smiles
B. Language Police
C. First Nations Freedom Fighters

192. What sweet dessert is made in Québec, is sold across Canada and is a hand-sized, chocolate-covered chocolate cake that has a layer of vanilla icing sandwiched in its centre?

A. Joe Louis Cakes
B. Beaver Tails
C. Poutine

193. Which of the following words is often used in Canada in place of "rubber bands"?

A. Eavestroughs
B. Condoms
C. Elastics

Answers 190 – 193

190. B. LCBO

Ontarians use either Liquor Store or LCBO interchangeably. LCBO actually stands for Liquor Control Board of Ontario. The LCBO runs more than 600 stores in Ontario and is one of the largest single purchasers of alcohol in the world, meaning that a lot of foreign booze imported into Ontario is rather cheap to buy.

191. B. Language Police

Truly, it is an Orwellian governmental body in the province of Québec that dictates the use of the French language. The Language Police are charged with ensuring that businesses in Québec use the French language on signs and in the workplace. There have been various challenges and modifications to the original scope of the Language Law, but it is still ensuring that French is used in Québec.

192. A. Joe Louis Cakes

These are extremely, one might even say, sickeningly, sweet and individually wrapped dessert cakes that are made in Québec and distributed throughout Canada. The cake was named after the sons of Arcade and Rose-Anna Vachon, the original makers of the cakes, not after the American boxer of a similar name. The cake's name is also pronounced "joe-lewy."

193. C. Elastics

Questions 194–197

194. Which British Columbia university is located in Burnaby, opened in 1965 and was designed by Arthur Erikson and Geoffrey Massey?

A. Simon Fraser University
B. University of British Columbia
C. University of Northern British Columbia

195. What is a more common term in Canada for silverware or flatware, as in knives, forks and spoons?

A. Broadsword
B. Cutlass
C. Cutlery

196. Which word is used at the end of a sentence with the purpose of turning a statement into a rhetorical question…and, of course, making the person using that word sound like a "knob" or a "hoser"?

A. Huh?
B. Right?
C. Eh?

197. Which of the following is a colloquial term for "Newfoundland"?

A. Lab East
B. The Squid
C. The Rock

Answers 194–197

194. A. Simon Fraser University

195. C. Cutlery

196. C. Eh?

197. C. The Rock

THE EDUCATION OF A CANADIAN,
ALONG WITH UNIQUELY CANADIAN WORDS

QUESTIONS 198 – 202

198. In which city would you find the main campus of the National Theatre School of Canada?
A. Montréal
B. Toronto
C. Ottawa

199. Which of the following exclamatory phrases is interchangeable with "Goddamn!"?
A. Eh!
B. Oh yeah!
C. Jesus Murphy!

200. Which of the following universities is not located in Manitoba?
A. Brandon University
B. Mount Allison University
C. University of Winnipeg

201. What is the name of the only university in Prince Edward Island?
A. University of Charlottetown
B. University of Prince Edward Island
C. Anne's Green Gables U and Dinner Theatre

202. Which word do some Canadians use interchangeably with the word "electricity"?
A. Hydro
B. Metro
C. Gas

Answers 198–202

198. A. Montréal

199. C. Jesus Murphy!

200. B. Mount Allison University
Its main campus is in Sackville, New Brunswick.

201. B. University of Prince Edward Island
It's in Charlottetown.

202. A. Hydro
Some Canadians refer to their electric bill as their "hydro bill." If the power goes out, they say "the hydro is out." The word comes from the short form of the Hydro-Electric Commission of Ontario.

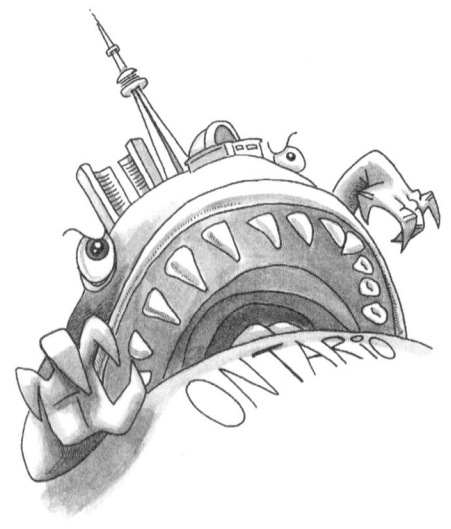

QUESTIONS 203 – 206

203. What Canadian university is located in Kingston, Ontario, and has the motto "Truth, Duty and Valour"?
A. Queen's University
B. Trent University
C. Royal Military College

204. What is the Canadian equivalent of the American "candy bar"?
A. Candy cane
B. Chocolate bar
C. Power bar

205. Which of the following words means something that Canadians use to pay their bills?
A. Cheque
B. Check
C. Czech

206. Which of the following words is interchangeable with "parking garage"?
A. Chump car chuck
B. ATM
C. Parkade

Answers 203 – 206

203. C. Royal Military College

Royal Military College (RMC) opened in June 1876 with a class of 18. The title "Royal" was granted by Queen Victoria in 1878. Since 1880, graduates have served in the North-West Rebellion of 1885, in the South African War, on the North-West Frontier of India, in World War I and II and in Korea, as well as participating in Canada's peacekeeping missions worldwide.

204. B. Chocolate bar

205. A. Cheque

"Check" is something you do, as in "Check to see if you have forgotten your keys," and "Czech" denotes somebody from the former Czech Republic.

206. C. Parkade

THE EDUCATION OF A CANADIAN,
ALONG WITH UNIQUELY CANADIAN WORDS

Questions 207 – 210

207. Which of the following is a modified member of the rapeseed family that Canadians have turned into extremely healthy cooking oil?
  A. Canola
  B. Olive
  C. Tar sand

208. The athletic teams of which Alberta university go by the name Dinos?
  A. University of Drumheller
  B. University of Calgary
  C. University of Camrose

209. How do Canadians pronounce the last letter of the alphabet?
  A. "Zee"
  B. "Why"
  C. "Zed"

210. Which of the following is the name of a species of land-locked salmon found in British Columbia as well as a brand of beer?
  A. Labatt's Blue
  B. Kokanee
  C. Foster's

207. A. Canola

208. B. University of Calgary

There is no university in Drumheller; and in Camrose, the institution of higher education is actually called Augustana University College.

209. C. "Zed"

The last letter of the alphabet is pronounced "zed" and rhymes with "said," in Canada. If you say "zee," you'll be understood, but you'll also get funny looks.

210. B. Kokanee

This brand of beer was originally just produced in British Colombia, but is now distributed elsewhere in Canada.

Questions 211–214

211. Which of the following describes a place where wacky, drug-induced people live in a happy state of haze while they constantly work at playing—or in other words, a colloquial term for British Columbia?

A. The Rock
B. The Soo
C. Lotus Land

212. Which Ontario university is located in Thunder Bay?

A. Trent University
B. Lakehead University
C. Laurentian University

213. What's the name of the original French colony in North America and is also how a select group of people in the East refer to themselves?

A. Acadian
B. Ontarian
C. Louisbourger

214. Which of the following slang terms does *not* mean a 40-ounce bottle of spirits (whiskey, rum, vodka, etc.)?

A. 40-pounder
B. 40-ouncer
C. 40 acres and a mule

ANSWERS 211 – 214

211. C. Lotus Land

It especially refers to the wackiest part of British Columbia, the lower mainland!

212. B. Lakehead University

213. A. Acadian

The original French colony in North America was called Acadia and encompassed everything from the Atlantic Ocean to the St. Lawrence, meaning Nova Scotia, New Brunswick, Prince Edward Island, southeastern Québec and even part of Maine. When the French-British battles over North America were finally settled, the French got booted, and the British decided they couldn't trust anyone who didn't swear an oath of allegiance to Britain. The Acadians were dispersed all over North America, and the best known group eventually settled in Louisiana where their descendants became known as Cajuns.

214. C. 40 acres and a mule

Both 40-pounder and 40-ouncer are used interchangeably to mean a 40-ounce bottle of spirits.

QUESTIONS 215–218

215. What word was common in the 1970s and used by ordinary folk to describe government money handed out to the unemployed?

A. Popey
B. Blarney
C. Pogey

216. Where is Acadia University located?

A. New Brunswick
B. Prince Edward Island
C. Nova Scotia

217. What is the American equivalent of what Canadians call "ham," or perhaps "back bacon"?

A. Prime rib
B. Pork chops
C. Canadian bacon

218. What is the colloquial term for the two-dollar coin in Canada?

A. Loonie
B. Toonie
C. Dabloonie

Answers 215–218

215. C. Pogey

It's now more commonly referred to as UI (Unemployment Insurance) or EI (Employment Insurance).

216. C. Nova Scotia

Specifically, it is in Wolfville, Nova Scotia.

217. C. Canadian bacon

There is no good explanation as to why Americans use this term, though they refer to Canadian bacon with fondness.

218. B. Toonie

It replaced the two-dollar paper bill in the 1990s. Toonies got their name only because they rhyme with loonie (the slang name given to the one-dollar coin). Toonies are slightly larger than loonies and are bimetallic, which means they have an outer ring that is silver in colour and the centre is copper coloured. The Queen's profile is on one side of the toonie and a polar bear is on the other.

Questions 219–222

219. Which New Brunswick university was the first in the country to develop an undergraduate degree program in forestry?

A. University of New Brunswick at Fredericton
B. St. Thomas University
C. Lansbridge University

220. Which university was formerly called "Collège du Sacré Coeur de Sudbury"?

A. Laval University
B. Laurentian University
C. Carleton University

221. Which word means "a narrow sled that is curled up at one end"?

A. Toboggan
B. Bombardier
C. Snowmobile

222. What blows across the plains of North America bringing frigid temperatures, disdain from Americans and, well, a whole lot of windy weather?

A. Chinook
B. Perfect storm
C. Alberta clipper

WHAT IS CANADA?

ANSWERS 219 – 222

219. A. University of New Brunswick at Fredericton

220. B. Laurentian University

221. A. Toboggan

222. C. Alberta clipper

QUESTIONS 223 – 226

223. Which of the following words is the name brand of a candy-coated chocolate that resembles, though doesn't taste like, plain M&Ms?
   A. Peanut M&Ms
   B. Smarties
   C. Nibs

224. In which city would you find the University of Alberta?
   A. Calgary
   B. Lethbridge
   C. Edmonton

225. What two-word phrase is the most common way that Ontarians refer to the Brewer's Retail?
   A. Liquor store
   B. Candy store
   C. Beer store

226. Which word is used by Canadians to describe something that hangs from the roof of house and catches rain and snow run-off and carries it to the ground?
   A. Eavestrough
   B. Clap trap
   C. Weird Harold

ANSWERS 223 – 226

223. B. Smarties

224. C. Edmonton

225. C. Beer store

In Ontario, breweries pooled their resources and set up outlets from which consumers could buy beer. Many different brands of beer in various sizes are available at the beer store. You can also purchase beer in liquor stores in Ontario, but there isn't nearly the selection of brands or quantities.

226. A. Eavestrough

Many Americans refer to this as "gutter."

227. The first Canadian medical school opened in 1824 and later became part of what Québec university?
   A. Bishop's University
   B. McGill University
   C. University of Toronto

228. Which of the following words denotes a big dinosaur resembling the *Tyrannosaurus rex*, yet slightly smaller?
   A. *Stegosaurus*
   B. *Kleinosaurus*
   C. *Albertosaurus*

229. What is the term for deeply meaningful and very, very, very "important" Canadian literature?
   A. Sleep inducing
   B. Can-Lit
   C. Bargain-bin sell-off

230. What is the Canadian equivalent of an American zip code?
   A. Zip code
   B. Postal code
   C. Nuisance letters

231. What are the centre parts of a donut sold as at Tim Hortons?
   A. Coffee
   B. Timbits
   C. Donut Holes

227. B. McGill University

228. C. *Albertosaurus*

The remains of *Albertosaurus* were discovered in the province of Alberta by Joseph Tyrrell in 1884 in an area called the Badlands, not because they were rebel-like, but because they were generally inhospitable. Don't you hate it when geographical areas don't have manners?

229. B. Can-Lit

230. B. Postal code

It contains six alpha-numeric characters, with a space after the third character, in this form: M4Y 1L6

231. B. Timbits

Instead of wasting the centre part of the donut, Tim Hortons turned them into round donut balls they call Timbits.

PROFESSIONAL SPORTS OF THE CANADIAN VARIETY

Sports, of the athletic variety, Canadian or otherwise, aren't really my favourite subject, though in writing about them, I am always amazed at the talent of a great many individuals. I am also amazed at the incredible monetary value placed on that talent—especially since there is really no correlation between money and talent in any other arena of Canadian society. So for those of you who just must have a crack at showing your superior knowledge in all things of a sporting nature, this chapter provides a start. In Chapter Ten you'll get a crack at sports of an amateur, semi-pro nature and even those of Olympic proportions. But for now, we'll stick to the pros...the Joes come later.

232. In what stadium did the CFL's Argonauts begin playing their home games in 1989?
- A. Skydome
- B. Varsity Stadium
- C. CNE Stadium

233. In the 1981–82 season, what Edmonton Oiler scored 92 goals in 80 games?
- A. Mario Lemieux
- B. Wayne Gretzky
- C. Paul Coffey

Answers 232 – 233

232. A. Skydome

233. B. Wayne Gretzky

PROFESSIONAL SPORTS OF THE CANADIAN VARIETY

Questions 234 – 238

234. In what venue was the first Grey Cup game played indoors way back in 1983?

A. Olympic Stadium Montréal
B. BC Place
C. Skydome

235. In what stadium do the Toronto Argonauts play their home games in 2008?

A. Skydome
B. CNE Stadium
C. Rogers Centre

236. What is the name of Hamilton's current CFL team?

A. Alouettes
B. Argonauts
C. Tiger-Cats

237. Which goalie was the youngest NHL player to ever win the Conn Smythe trophy?

A. Jacques Plante
B. Tony Esposito
C. Patrick Roy

238. How many times did Wayne Gretzky win the NHL's Most Valuable Player award in the 1980s?

A. Six
B. Nine
C. Ten

234. B. BC Place
In beautiful Vancouver, of course.

235. C. Rogers Centre
Since Rogers bought Skydome a few years back and changed the name, the Argos now play in Rogers Centre, though the building remains the same old Skydome.

236. C. Tiger-Cats

237. C. Patrick Roy
He won the trophy at age 20 in 1986.

238. B. Nine
He won MVP in the years 1979–87 and in 1989.

QUESTIONS 239 – 243

239. What number did Frank Mahovlich wear as a Toronto Maple Leaf, a Detroit Red Wing and a Montréal Canadien?

A. 12
B. 27
C. 33

240. Which NHL player was born in Mitchell, Ontario, and dubbed the "Babe Ruth of Hockey"?

A. Howie Morenz
B. Bobby Hull
C. Bobby Orr

241. For most of the 20th century, what arena was home to the NHL's Canadiens?

A. Molson Centre
B. Montréal Arena
C. Montréal Forum

242. What is the name of Montréal's current CFL team?

A. Concorde
B. Vingt-Deux
C. Alouettes

243. What retired left wing hockey player is known as the Golden Jet?

A. Bobby Orr
B. Bobby Hull
C. Bobby Clark

Answers 239 – 243

239. B. 27

240. A. Howie Morenz

241. C. Montréal Forum

It was home to the NHL's Montréal Maroons from 1924 to 1938 and the Montréal Canadiens from 1926 to 1996. The Canadian Arena Company built the Forum in 159 days. It was rebuilt in 1968 and occupied until 1996.

242. C. Alouettes

The Montréal team was briefly called Concorde (1983–87), and then the city was without a team for nine years. The Alouettes returned to Montréal in 1996. The CFL team from Baltimore (The Stallions) moved north and took up residence in Montréal under the old but glorious name of Alouettes.

243. B. Bobby Hull

He was nicknamed "Golden Jet" because of his blond hair and blinding speed!

PROFESSIONAL SPORTS OF THE CANADIAN VARIETY

QUESTIONS 244 – 248

244. In 1989, which goalie was the first Soviet hockey player to be inducted into the Hockey Hall of Fame?
   A. Evgeni Malkin
   B. Alexander Ovechkin
   C. Vladislav Tretiak

245. Which hockey player is nicknamed "The Great One"?
   A. Wayne Gretzky
   B. Phil Esposito
   C. Bobby Orr

246. What is the nickname of NHL player Curtis Joseph?
   A. Tis
   B. Cujo
   C. Kurt

247. In what pro sport are the Norris and Jennings trophies awarded?
   A. Football
   B. Baseball
   C. Hockey

248. What NHL trophy is given to the most valuable player in the playoffs?
   A. Art Ross Trophy
   B. Bill Masterson Trophy
   C. Conn Smythe Trophy

244. C. Vladislav Tretiak

He is considered one of the greatest goaltenders in the history of ice hockey. Tretiak became head of the Russian Ice Hockey Federation on April 25, 2006—his 54th birthday.

245. A. Wayne Gretzky

246. B. Cujo

247. C. Hockey

The Norris Trophy is given to the outstanding defence player in each season and is named for James Norris, the late former owner and president of the Detroit Red Wings. The Jennings Trophy is awarded to the goaltender with the least number of goals scored against him during the regular season. It is named for William M. Jennings, a longtime governor and president of the New York Rangers.

248. C. Conn Smythe Trophy

Winners are selected by the Professional Hockey Writers' Association. The late Conn Smythe was a coach, manager, president and owner-governor of the Toronto Maple Leafs.

Questions 249–252

249. What professional sport is Steve Nash associated with?
- A. Baseball
- B. Basketball
- C. Football

250. What is the name of Ottawa's current CFL team?
- A. Roughriders
- B. Senators
- C. Renegades

251. Bret "Hitman" Hart competed in the WWF, which is a professional league where athletes compete in what sport?
- A. Football
- B. Wrestling
- C. Acting

252. What sport is Jacques Villeneuve associated with?
- A. Hockey
- B. Car racing
- C. Chuck wagon racing

ANSWERS 249–252

249. B. Basketball

Born in Canada, Nash plays point guard for the Phoenix Suns.

250. None of the above

It's a trick question, because Ottawa does not currently have a CFL team. The last team was called the Renegades and lasted from 2002 to 2005. Ottawa was without a CFL franchise from 1996 to 2002. Prior to that, Ottawa's team was called the Rough Riders.

251. B. Wrestling

Some of you may have chosen "Acting" as the sport of the WWF (World Wrestling Federation). Though, to be fair, most professional sports do involve an element of acting. Bret "Hitman" Hart was born in Calgary into the wrestling Hart family. As a wrestler, he also used the names Brett Hart, Buddy "The Heartthrob" Hart, and "Cowboy" Brett Hart. He was a two-time World Champion Wresting Heavyweight Champion and five-time WWF Champion. Hart was inducted into the World Wresting Entertainment (WWE) Hall of Fame in 2006 by another famous wrestler, Stone Cold Steve Austin. (WWF became the WWE in 2002, resolving an ongoing dispute with the other WWF—World Wildlife Fund.) Hart was also inducted into the Professional Wrestling Hall of Fame (in Amsterdam, New York) as part of the class of 2008.

252. B. Car racing

Son of the late Formula One driver Gilles Villeneuve, Jacques was born in St-Jean-sur-Richelieu, Québec, in 1971. He has driven at CART, NASCAR and Formula One.

QUESTIONS 253–257

253. Who was the first Canadian to win the Masters Golf Tournament?
A. Dave Barr
B. Mike Weir
C. Al Balding

254. In what Canadian city would you find the Hockey Hall of Fame?
A. Toronto
B. Montréal
C. Vancouver

255. What was the only team to win back-to-back World Series in the 1990s?
A. Braves
B. Blue Jays
C. Expos

256. What professional sport do athletes compete in for the NLL?
A. Luge
B. Lacrosse
C. Lawn bowling

257. What is the name of Toronto's current CFL team?
A. Royals
B. Argonauts
C. Blue Jays

Answers 253 – 257

253. B. Mike Weir

He was born in Sarnia, Ontario, in 1970 and spent more than 100 weeks in the top 10 of the World Golf Official Rankings from 2001 to 2005. He won the Masters in 2003.

254. A. Toronto

255. B. Blue Jays

In 1992 the Toronto Blue Jays defeated Atlanta; in 1993 they defeated Philadelphia.

256. B. Lacrosse

The National Lacrosse League (NLL) is the professional indoor men's lacrosse league that, unlike most other lacrosse leagues, plays its games in winter. The league began its 22nd season in December 2007. Teams compete for the Champion's Cup. There are currently 12 teams, with three based in Canada (Calgary Roughnecks, Edmonton Rush, Toronto Rock) and nine based in the U.S. (Buffalo Bandits, Chicago Shamrox, Colorado Mammoth, Minnesota Swarm, New York Titans, Philadelphia Wings, Portland Lumberjax, Rochester Knighthawks, San Jose Stealth). The Rochester Knighthawks were league champions in 2007.

257. B. Argonauts

PROFESSIONAL SPORTS OF THE CANADIAN VARIETY

QUESTIONS 258 – 262

258. On November 22, 2003, what two teams faced off in Commonwealth Stadium in the first-ever NHL regular season game held outdoors?
A. Winnipeg and Toronto
B. Edmonton and Calgary
C. Edmonton and Montréal

259. Which hockey player was named the NHL's Most Valuable Player nine times in the 1980s?
A. Paul Coffey
B. Jari Kurri
C. Wayne Gretzky

260. In the Montréal Forum, what did the letters "CH" at centre ice stand for?
A. Club de Hockey Canadien
B. Champions
C. Champlain

261. In what Canadian city would your find the Canadian Football Hall of Fame?
A. Hamilton
B. Toronto
C. Ottawa

262. Which two Alberta premiers once played football for the Edmonton Eskimos?
A. Stelmach and Klein
B. Manning and Aberhart
C. Lougheed and Getty

258. C. Edmonton and Montréal

The Montréal Canadiens won 4–3.

259. C. Wayne Gretzky

260. A. Club de Hockey Canadien

261. A. Hamilton

It celebrates great achievements in Canadian football, not just in the Canadian Football League.

262. C. Lougheed and Getty

Peter Lougheed played for the Eskimos for two seasons (1949 and 1950); Don Getty played for the Eskimos for 10 years during the 1950s and '60s and led them to two Grey Cup wins, in 1955 and 1956.

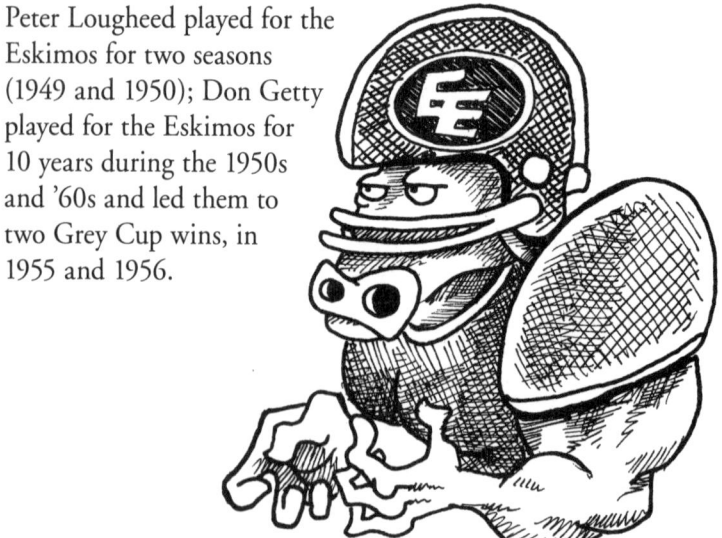

Questions 263 – 266

263. Which team has won the Stanley Cup the most times from 1918 to 2007?
A. Montréal Canadiens
B. Toronto Maple Leafs
C. Edmonton Oilers

264. In the NHL, what trophy is awarded to the best defensive forward?
A. King Clancy Trophy
B. Lady Byng Trophy
C. Selke Trophy

265. What is the name of Vancouver's current CFL team?
A. BC Pandas
B. Vancouver Canucks
C. BC Lions

266. What NHL trophy is awarded for sportsmanship?
A. Lady Byng Trophy
B. President's Trophy
C. Vezina Trophy

Answers 263–266

263. A. Montréal Canadiens

They won the Stanley Cup 24 times. The top 10 teams to win the Stanley Cup during the NHL era from 1918 to the present:

- Montréal Canadiens, 24
- Toronto Maple Leafs, 11, or 13*
- Detroit Red Wings, 10
- Ottawa Senators, 6
- Boston Bruins, 5
- Edmonton Oilers, 5
- New York Rangers, 4
- New York Islanders, 4
- Chicago Blackhawks, 3
- New Jersey Devils, 2

*Pre-NHL, there were a whole host of other teams that went by various names. The Toronto Maple Leafs had 11 wins; however, the Toronto Arenas won the cup in 1918, and the Toronto St. Pats won the cup in 1922. Most statisticians lob the three teams together, but as you can see, I've explained the discrepancy for you.

264. C. Selke Trophy

The winner is selected by the Professional Hockey Writers' Association. The trophy is named for Frank Selke, who is considered one of the great architects of NHL championship teams. Selke was general manager of both the Toronto Maple Leafs and the Montréal Canadiens at different times during his career.

265. C. BC Lions

266. A. Lady Byng Trophy

QUESTIONS 267 – 271

267. What is the only U.S.-based team to have won the Grey Cup?
A. Las Vegas Posse
B. Memphis Mad Dogs
C. Baltimore Stallions

268. Which trophy is awarded each year to the most outstanding rookie in the NHL?
A. Prince of Wales Trophy
B. Calder Trophy
C. Maurice Richard Trophy

269. What is currently the only NBA team based in Canada?
A. Vancouver Grizzlies
B. Toronto Raptors
C. Montréal Nuggets

270. What trophy is awarded to the player who scores the most goals in each NHL season?
A. Lester Patrick Trophy
B. Jack Adams Award
C. Maurice Richard Trophy

271. Which goalie became the first woman to be signed by an NHL team?
A. Hayley Wickenheiser
B. Manon Rheaume
C. Cathy Phillips

267. C. Baltimore Stallions

They were based in Baltimore, Maryland, and in the two seasons they competed in the league, they made it to the Grey Cup final both times. In the 1994 final they were beaten 26–23 by the BC Lions in BC Place Stadium in Vancouver. In 1995, the Stallions defeated the Calgary Stampeders at Regina's Taylor Field, 37–20.

268. B. Calder Trophy

Frank Calder was the NHL's president from 1936 until his death in 1943.

269. B. Toronto Raptors

They've been playing the pro version of the game in Toronto since 1995.

270. C. Maurice Richard Trophy

The trophy is donated by the Montréal Canadiens to the NHL in memory of Maurice "The Rocket" Richard, the first player to score 50 goals in 50 games, 50 goals in a season, and 500 goals in a career.

271. B. Manon Rheaume

She was also the first woman to play in the NHL, since she played two exhibition games for the Tampa Bay Lightning in 1992.

Questions 272–275

272. What is the name of Edmonton's current CFL team?
  A. Stampeders
  B. Roughriders
  C. Eskimos

273. What trophy is given to the victors of the seven-game series between the NHL's Eastern Conference Champions and Western Conference Champions?
  A. Clarence Campbell Bowl
  B. Prince of Wales Trophy
  C. Stanley Cup

274. Which one of the following was not part of the "Original Six" NHL teams that existed before the 1967 NHL expansion?
  A. Ottawa Senators
  B. Toronto Maple Leafs
  C. Chicago Blackhawks

275. What is the name of Calgary's current CFL team?
  A. Blue Bombers
  B. Stampeders
  C. Schooners

ANSWERS 272 – 275

272. C. Eskimos

273. C. Stanley Cup

274. A. Ottawa Senators
The original six were the Montréal Canadiens, Toronto Maple Leafs, Boston Bruins, Detroit Red Wings, New York Rangers and Chicago Blackhawks.

275. B. Stampeders

Questions 276 – 280

276. What has an NHL player accomplished if he is awarded the Art Ross Trophy?
A. Top scorer in the playoffs
B. Most valuable player
C. Top point scorer in the regular season

277. For what accomplishment does an NHL player receive the Vezina Trophy?
A. Best goaltender
B. Top goal scorer
C. Most valuable player

278. What is the name of Winnipeg's current CFL team?
A. Tiger-Cats
B. Blue Bombers
C. Argonauts

279. Who presently leads the NHL for goals scored in the regular season?
A. Marcel Dionne
B. Gordie Howe
C. Wayne Gretzky

280. What is the name of Regina's current CFL team?
A. Regina Rams
B. Saskatchewan Roughriders
C. Moose Jaw Buffalos

276. C. Top point scorer in the regular season

Arthur Howie Ross was the former manager and coach of the Boston Bruins.

277. A. Best goaltender

The best goaltender is decided by a vote of the general managers of all NHL teams. Leo Dandurand, Louis Letourneau and Joe Cattarinich presented the trophy to the NHL in 1926–27 in memory of Georges Vezina, an outstanding goalkeeper for the Montréal Canadiens. Vezina collapsed during an NHL game in 1925 and died of tuberculosis a short time later.

278. C. Argonauts

279. C. Wayne Gretzky

Gretzky still leads the NHL with 894 goals scored in the regular season. Gordie Howe is second with 801 goals scored in the regular season. Gretzky holds or shares 61 NHL records.

280. B. Saskatchewan Roughriders

Questions 281 – 284

281. Which goaltender holds the record for most NHL regular-season wins?

A. Curtis Joseph
B. Terry Sawchuk
C. Patrick Roy

282. Which CFL team has competed in the Grey Cup final more than all other teams?

A. Edmonton
B. Hamilton
C. Montréal

283. Which team has won the Grey Cup more than all others?

A. Toronto
B. Edmonton
C. Winnipeg

284. Which year saw the most fumbles in a Grey Cup game?

A. 1986 (Edmonton and Hamilton)
B. 1991 (Toronto and Calgary)
C. 1965 (Hamilton and Winnipeg)

281. C. Patrick Roy

Roy leads the NHL with 551 regular season wins. Martin Brodeaur ranks second with 529.

282. A. Edmonton

The top five with the most number of appearances in the Grey Cup final are:
- Edmonton Eskimos, 24
- Winnipeg Blue Bombers, 22
- Toronto Argonauts, 21
- Hamilton Tiger-Cats, 18
- Montréal Alouettes, 16

(Statistics based on the years 1909–2007)

283. A. Toronto

The top five with the most Grey Cup wins are:
- Toronto Argonauts, 15
- Edmonton Eskimos, 13
- Winnipeg Blue Bombers, 10
- Ottawa Rough Riders, 9
- Montréal Alouettes, 6

(Statistics based on the years 1909–2007)

284. A. 1986 (Edmonton and Hamilton)

There were seven fumbles. (Statistics for 1959–2007)

Questions 285–287

285. What NBA team was based in Vancouver from 1995 to 2001 and subsequently moved to Memphis?

A. Ottawa Senators
B. Vancouver Grizzlies
C. Toronto Raptors

286. What is the only Canadian city that currently has a Major League Baseball franchise?

A. Montréal
B. Vancouver
C. Toronto

287. What Canadian-born auto racer is nicknamed "The Thrill from West Hill"?

A. Paul Tracy
B. Ross Bentley
C. Patrick Carpentier

Answers 285 – 287

285. B. Vancouver Grizzlies

286. C. Toronto

The Toronto Blue Jays are currently the only MLB team in Canada. The Montréal Expos existed as a MLB team from 1969 to 2004. They were then relocated to Washington, DC, and renamed the Washington Nationals. Although the Expos never won the World Series, they did win their Eastern Division title in 1981 defeating the Philadelphia Phillies. They went on to the National League Championship Series, where they were defeated by the Los Angeles Dodgers who eventually became World Series Champions that year when they defeated the New York Yankees.

287. A. Paul Tracy

He was born in Scarborough, Ontario, in 1968. When he was 16 years old, Tracy became the youngest Canadian Formula Ford Champion. In 1986 he became the youngest winner of the single seater Can-Am series. He is probably best known for competing in Champ Car competitions for Penske and Newman/Haas, Team KOOL Green, and Player's Forsythe. In 2003, while driving for Player's Forsythe, Tracy became the first driver in 32 years to win the first three races of the season (in St. Petersburg, Monterrey and Long Beach). That same year, he won at Toronto (where he led all 112 laps), Vancouver, Mid-Ohio and Mexico City. He also won his first-ever championship that year. Since then, Tracy's career has been spotty at best.

CANADIAN GEOGRAPHY WITH SOME ODDITIES THROWN IN FOR GOOD MEASURE

Testing your geographical knowledge is a great way to discover how deluded you are about how much you know. Then again, in a vast country such as Canada, how could you expect to know everything? Pronouncing many of Canada's place names is at the very least challenging. But hey, if you didn't want a challenge, you surely wouldn't have purchased this page turner!

As an added challenge, try to answer all the questions before you look at the answers. Or, for an even greater challenge, read the answers first and try to determine the questions. People at parties love to be challenged like this. So go ahead and bring this chapter out at your next soirée. Then you'll never have to hold another soirée again. Unless you move, in which case you can start this wholly divisive geographical challenge over again!

288. Where in Ontario is the southernmost point on Canada's mainland?

A. Windsor
B. Fort Erie
C. Point Pelee

289. In what Ontario town would you find a former Cold War bunker that's now a museum and lovingly called the "Diefenbunker"?

A. Carp
B. Nepean
C. Kingston

WHAT IS CANADA?

ANSWERS 288 – 289

288. C. Point Pelee

289. A. Carp

It is 35 kilometres east of Ottawa, and the Diefenbunker was in use up until 1994. It was built to protect Canada's very important people (prime ministers and hangers-on, no doubt) in case of nuclear war.

CANADIAN GEOGRAPHY WITH SOME ODDITIES THROWN IN FOR GOOD MEASURE

QUESTIONS 290 – 294

290. In which Canadian province is there a town named Truro within a county called Colchester?
 A. Newfoundland
 B. Nova Scotia
 C. Prince Edward Island

291. In which province would you find Grand Lake, Red Indian Lake and Gander Lake?
 A. Newfoundland and Labrador
 B. Ontario
 C. Manitoba

292. What province is the supposed location of the fabled Lost Lemon Mine...although it is still lost?
 A. British Columbia
 B. Alberta
 C. Ontario

293. Which is the highest waterfall (measured by its vertical drop) in Canada?
 A. Niagara Falls, Ontario
 B. Hunlen Falls, BC
 C. Della Falls, BC

294. What lake is part of the waterway connecting Lake Huron to Lake Erie?
 A. Lake St. Clair
 B. Lake of the Woods
 C. Lake Charles

290. B. Nova Scotia

Truro was settled in 1761 and is in central Nova Scotia.

291. A. Newfoundland and Labrador

292. B. Alberta

The Lost Lemon Mine is supposed to be chock-full of gold and is perhaps located somewhere near the Crowsnest Pass. The search for the mine has led to misery and death more than a few times, though on occasion, some nut runs down from the hills and claims he's found it. Then loses it.

293. C. Della Falls, BC

Della Falls, Della Lake, BC, is Canada's highest waterfalls at 440 metres. Second is Takakkaw Falls, Daly Glacier, BC, at 254 metres, and third is Hunlen Falls, at Atnarko River, BC, at 253 metres. For those of you who can't believe Niagara Falls isn't the highest, it doesn't even fall within the top 10; it is only 53 metres in height.

294. A. Lake St. Clair

Along with the Detroit River and St. Clair River, Lake St. Clair connects Lake Huron to Lake Erie.

CANADIAN GEOGRAPHY WITH SOME ODDITIES THROWN IN FOR GOOD MEASURE

Questions 295 – 298

---

295. What is Canada's easternmost point?
  A. Cape of Good Hope, New Brunswick
  B. Cape Spear, Newfoundland
  C. Points East, Nunavut

296. Which lake in southwestern Ontario is named after Upper Canada's first lieutenant-governor?
  A. Lake Huron
  B. Lake Simcoe
  C. Bobs Lake

297. On what tiny Nova Scotia island have people been trying to find buried treasure in a so-called Money Pit for more than 200 years?
  A. Oak Island
  B. Cape Breton Island
  C. Campobello Island

298. Founded in 1790, what is the major seaport for Prince Edward Island's potato industry?
  A. Summerside
  B. Charlottetown
  C. Green Gables

ANSWERS 295 – 298

295. B. Cape Spear, Newfoundland

296. B. Lake Simcoe
Lake Simcoe is named for John Graves Simcoe, Upper Canada's lieutenant-governor from 1791 to 1798.

297. A. Oak Island
Oak Island is a very small island that lies in Mahone Bay on Nova Scotia's eastern shore. In 1795 a teenager tripped over a circular depression on the island, which strangely enough was directly beneath a tree with cut branches that looked as if they'd been used as a pulley. The young lad and two of his friends dug up the ground under the tree with thoughts of Captain Kidd's treasure in their youthful noggins. As they dug, they hit ingeniously placed flagstones and various layers of logs. They abandoned their excavating but returned a number of years later with a corporation in tow to help them. As they dug deeper they uncovered a stone inscribed with "mysterious writing" and more logs. Then just as they thought they were getting close, the hole filled up with seawater. They cried "booby trap," and the tall tale grew from there. Over the years many people have tried to figure out how to get around the "booby traps," but to no avail. Oak Island still won't give up what is at the bottom of the "money pit." Probably a banker.

298. A. Summerside

Questions 299 – 302

299. In what "green-blooded" Alberta town would you find a replica starship *Enterprise* along with a tourism and Trek station?

A. St. Paul
B. Vulcan
C. Kirk

300. What Canadian island has the largest total surface area?

A. Ellesmere Island
B. Victoria Island
C. Baffin Island

301. What national park contains the largest icefield in the Canadian Rockies?

A. Jasper National Park
B. Yoho National Park
C. Glacier National Park

302. What national park has Yukon's largest lake and Canada's highest peak?

A. Vuntut National Park
B. Ivvavik National Park
C. Kluane National Park

WHAT IS CANADA?

ANSWERS 299 – 302

299. B. Vulcan

The Vulcan Tourism and Trek Station is a tourist information centre that has cleverly capitalized on its name in connection with the home planet of a character from a TV show with rabidly loyal fans. *Star Trek*'s Mr. Spock was from the planet Vulcan, and he had green blood (that was my clever clue in the question, get it?). The Tourism and Trek Centre consists of a main building that looks like a landing pad, in addition to a replica *Star Trek* ship. Each June the town even hosts a Trek-related festival that draws *Star Trek* fans from far and wide.

300. C. Baffin Island

Canada's three largest islands are Baffin Island (507,451 km^2), Victoria Island (217,291 km^2) and Ellesmere Island (196,236 km^2).

301. A. Jasper National Park

Athabasca Glacier is found in Jasper and is the largest icefield in the Canadian Rockies as well as the largest icefield south of Alaska. Jasper is the largest of Canada's national parks in the Rocky Mountains.

302. C. Kluane National Park

It is in the extreme southwestern corner of Yukon. As for the identities of Canada's largest lake and highest peak, those questions are coming up.

CANADIAN GEOGRAPHY WITH SOME ODDITIES
THROWN IN FOR GOOD MEASURE

QUESTIONS 303 – 307

303. In which of the following places would you not find the world's largest turtle statue?
   A. Turtleford, Saskatchewan
   B. Turtle Island, Ontario
   C. Boissevain, Manitoba

304. What city is the home base of Canada's precision flying team, the Snowbirds?
   A. Gimli, Manitoba
   B. Moose Jaw, Saskatchewan
   C. Cold Lake, Alberta

305. Which capital city was once called Bytown?
   A. Ottawa
   B. Toronto
   C. Québec City

306. What Canadian province has the smallest land area and population?
   A. Prince Edward Island
   B. New Brunswick
   C. Nova Scotia

307. Which of the five Great Lakes has the smallest surface area?
   A. Lake Erie
   B. Lake Huron
   C. Lake Ontario

Answers 303 – 307

303. B. Turtle Island, Ontario

Both Turtleford, Saskatchewan, and Boissevain, Manitoba, have statues depicting very large turtles that measure 8.5 metres from beak to tail.

304. B. Moose Jaw, Saskatchewan

CFB Moose Jaw is home base for the Snowbirds, whose official designation is Canadian Forces 431 Air Demonstration Squadron. For bonus points, do you know what aircraft are flown by Snowbirds pilots? CT-114 Tutors.

305. A. Ottawa

Bytown was named for Colonel John By, a British officer who was instrumental in building the Rideau Canal. Bytown was incorporated as a city in 1855, at which time its name was changed to Ottawa.

306. A. Prince Edward Island

307. C. Lake Ontario

CANADIAN GEOGRAPHY WITH SOME ODDITIES THROWN IN FOR GOOD MEASURE

Questions 308 – 311

308. Which province grows a lot of potatoes and has a beach where the sand has been known to "sing"?
   A. Prince Edward Island
   B. New Brunswick
   C. Nova Scotia

309. What is the highest point in Nunavut?
   A. Outlook Peak
   B. Barbeau Peak
   C. Mount Odin

310. The largest part of the border between the United States and Canada lies along what parallel?
   A. 49th
   B. 38th
   C. 43rd

311. What Yukon city got its name from the local rapids on the Yukon River, which were said to look like the mane of an equine?
   A. Dawson City
   B. Whitehorse
   C. Ibex Valley

308. A. Prince Edward Island

Basin Head Beach on the eastern tip of the province is one of a few places on this great and wacky planet where the sand is known to "sing." More accurately, it squeaks. It has something to do with the quartz sand on the beach being extremely well rounded. Scientists say they don't really understand the phenomenon, so please do not shoot me, your lowly messenger. I wonder if the sands know "Moon River"?

309. B. Barbeau Peak

Barbeau Peak is 2616 metres. It is not only the highest point in Nunavut, but also the highest point in eastern North America as well as the highest point in the Arctic Archipelago.

310. A. 49th

The 49th parallel is the part of the border that extends from Manitoba to British Columbia. This border was settled on by the Oregon Treaty (1846).

311. B. Whitehorse

The rapids on the Yukon River apparently looked like the mane of a white horse. The rapids that provided the city's name are now submerged under Schwatka Lake, which was created when a hydro dam was built in the 1950s.

QUESTIONS 312–315

312. What is the highway number of the Macdonald–Cartier Freeway in Ontario?
  A. 400
  B. 401
  C. 403

313. In 1995, what Nova Scotia fishing port and birthplace of the schooner *Bluenose* was designated a UNESCO World Heritage Site?
  A. Truro
  B. Dartmouth
  C. Lunenburg

314. In what province would you find The Glass House, a home constructed out of embalming fluid bottles that overlooks Kootenay Lake?
  A. Alberta
  B. Manitoba
  C. British Columbia

315. In what territory was there a church shaped like an igloo in a place called Inuvik?
  A. Northwest Territories
  B. Yukon
  C. Nunavut

312. B. 401

In August 2007, the part of the 401 that extends from Trenton to the 404 in Toronto was given the additional name "Highway of Heroes," to honour Canadian Forces personnel who have been killed in Afghanistan.

313. C. Lunenburg

The town was founded in 1753 and was named for King George II of Great Britain who also ruled Brunswick-Lunenburg. The UNESCO designation is intended to protect the town's unique architecture and design, which are considered the best examples of planned British colonial settlement in North America.

314. C. British Columbia

The Glass House is in Boswell, BC, and was built by a retired mortician in the 1950s.

315. A. Northwest Territories

The Igloo Church, as it was commonly called, was officially Our Lady of Victory Roman Catholic Church. It was built in 1959–60, but unfortunately burned down last year. Funds are being raised and hopefully construction of the new igloo church will begin sometime in the fall of 2008.

CANADIAN GEOGRAPHY WITH SOME ODDITIES THROWN IN FOR GOOD MEASURE

Questions 316 – 320

316. In what eastern province would you find the Eastern Townships?
A. Ontario
B. Québec
C. New Brunswick

317. Which of the following is Canada's most populous city?
A. Toronto
B. Montréal
C. Vancouver

318. In which provincial capital would you find the Fairmont Empress Hotel?
A. Winnipeg
B. Regina
C. Victoria

319. What provincial capital is at the junction of the Red and Assiniboine rivers?
A. Winnipeg
B. Regina
C. Edmonton

320. What town merged with Port Arthur to become Thunder Bay, Ontario?
A. Port Elgin
B. Sudbury
C. Fort William

ANSWERS 316 – 320

316. B. Québec
The Eastern Townships are in southeastern Québec, squished between the original seigneuries south of the St. Lawrence River and the U.S. border.

317. A. Toronto
There are approximately 5.4 million people who live in Toronto, and it is not only Canada's most populous city, but also the fifth largest city in North America after Mexico City, New York City, Los Angeles and Chicago.

318. C. Victoria

319. A. Winnipeg

320. C. Fort William
They merged way back in 1970.

Questions 321–324

321. What Ontario city is near Hamilton and named for a Mohawk war chief who fought alongside the British during the American Revolution?

A. Burlington
B. Waterdown
C. Brantford

322. What hills form the highest point in Saskatchewan?

A. Regina Moll Hills
B. Saskatoon Hills
C. Cypress Hills

323. On what island would you find Sydney, Nova Scotia?

A. Campobello
B. Cape Breton
C. St. Pierre

324. In what Alberta town would you find the world's largest dinosaur replica?

A. Canmore
B. Drumheller
C. Calgary

ANSWERS 321 – 324

321. C. Brantford

The city was named for Joseph Brant, though it is probably most famous for a couple of other former residents: Wayne Gretzky and Alexander Graham Bell. It's often called the Telephone City because Bell invented the telephone, at least in part, while living at the Bell homestead just outside Brantford.

322. C. Cypress Hills

They are in the southwest corner of the province, and the highest point doesn't have an official name, but rises to a height of 1468 metres.

323. B. Cape Breton

324. B. Drumheller

The dino (a T-Rex) stands 25 metres tall and is 46 metres from head to tail. Visitors can climb the 106 stairs inside the dino and stop at the top on a viewing platform inside its mouth.

CANADIAN GEOGRAPHY WITH SOME ODDITIES THROWN IN FOR GOOD MEASURE

QUESTIONS 325 – 329

325. What national park reserve is located on the west coast of Vancouver Island?
  A. Torngat Mountains National Park Reserve
  B. Pacific Rim National Park Reserve
  C. Mingan Archipelago National Park Reserve

326. Which province is home to the world's largest pyrogy on a fork?
  A. Manitoba
  B. Saskatchewan
  C. Alberta

327. What is the highest mountain in Alberta?
  A. Mount Columbia
  B. Mushroom Peak
  C. Panther Mountain

328. What Manitoba town is the self-proclaimed "Capital of New Iceland"?
  A. Brandon
  B. Winnipeg
  C. Gimli

329. What is the more common name of southwestern Ontario's largest exposed bedrock structure?
  A. Ishpanina Ridge
  B. Sudbury
  C. Niagara Escarpment

ANSWERS 325 – 329

325. B. Pacific Rim National Park Reserve
Torngat Mountains National Park Reserve is in Labrador, and Mingan Archipelago National Park Reserve is in Québec.

326. C. Alberta
It's actually in Glendon, Alberta.

327. A. Mount Columbia
It is 3747 metres high and is also the second highest peak in the Canadian Rockies.

328. C. Gimli
It was founded in 1875 by settlers from Iceland.

329. C. Niagara Escarpment
In Hamilton, where I was born, we also referred to it as The Mountain.

CANADIAN GEOGRAPHY WITH SOME ODDITIES THROWN IN FOR GOOD MEASURE

QUESTIONS 330 – 334

330. In what river would you find Ontario's Thousand Islands?
A. St. Lawrence River
B. Lake St. Clair
C. Grand River

331. What is the highest point in Manitoba?
A. Badger on Hind Legs
B. Baldy Mountain
C. Birds Hill

332. Which province is the location of Fundy National Park?
A. New Brunswick
B. Prince Edward Island
C. Nova Scotia

333. In which baby of a territory would you find Auyuittuq National Park?
A. Northwest Territories
B. Yukon
C. Nunavut

334. What large roadside attraction in Vegreville, Alberta, is also referred to locally as the World's Largest Pysanka?
A. Outhouse
B. Moose
C. Easter egg

WHAT IS CANADA?

ANSWERS 330 – 334

330. A. St. Lawrence River
There are closer to 2000 islands in the Thousand Islands chain. Straddling the Canada-U.S. border near Kingston, Ontario, they vary in size from 100 km², down to small islands occupied by birds, and even smaller outcroppings of rock.

331. B. Baldy Mountain
It is 832 metres high and is 60 kilometres north of Dauphin in Duck Mountain Provincial Park.

332. A. New Brunswick

333. C. Nunavut

334. C. Easter egg
Vegreville's Easter egg is the largest of its kind. It measures 7 metres from top to bottom (9.4 metres tall including its base) and has a diameter of 5.5 metres. "Easter egg" in the Ukrainian language is "pysanka," and many residents of the town are descended from Ukrainian immigrants.

CANADIAN GEOGRAPHY WITH SOME ODDITIES THROWN IN FOR GOOD MEASURE

QUESTIONS 335 – 339

335. In which province would you find Gros Morne National Park?
A. British Columbia
B. Alberta
C. Newfoundland and Labrador

336. What is the highest mountain in British Columbia?
A. Fairweather Mountain
B. Mount Albert Edward
C. Mount Pierre Elliott Trudeau

337. What Yukon mountain is Canada's highest peak?
A. Mount Lucania
B. King Peak
C. Mount Logan

338. What is the longest river wholly within British Columbia?
A. Columbia River
B. Fraser River
C. South Saskatchewan River

339. Lake of the Woods is not located within which of the following provinces?
A. Québec
B. Ontario
C. Manitoba

335. C. Newfoundland and Labrador

336. A. Fairweather Mountain
It stands at 4663 metres and is at the southern end of the St. Elias Mountains.

337. C. Mount Logan
It is 5996 metres tall and is in Kluane National Park.

338. B. Fraser River
It is 1368 kilometres long and flows from Mount Robson in central BC into the Pacific Ocean at Vancouver.

339. A. Québec
Lake of the Woods is shared by Ontario, Manitoba and the U.S. state of Minnesota.

Canadian Geography with Some Oddities Thrown in for Good Measure

Questions 340–344

340. Channel-Port aux Basques is in which of the following provinces?
A. New Brunswick
B. Québec
C. Newfoundland and Labrador

341. Graham and Moresby islands are part of what British Columbian archipelago?
A. Mindinao
B. Queen Charlotte Islands
C. Aleutian Islands

342. Which territory in Canada has the largest total area?
A. Nunavut
B. Yukon
C. Northwest Territories

343. What is the highest point in New Brunswick?
A. Big Bald Mountain
B. Green Mountain
C. Mount Carleton

344. Which BC community is the home of the World's Largest Hockey Stick and Puck?
A. Nelson
B. 100 Mile House
C. Duncan

340. C. Newfoundland and Labrador
It is at the southwestern tip on the island of Newfoundland.

341. B. Queen Charlotte Islands
First Nations people call them Haida Gwaii, which translates to "Islands of the People."

342. A. Nunavut
It covers 2,093,190 km² and comprises 21 percent of Canada.

343. C. Mount Carleton
It stands 817 metres tall and is in Mount Carleton Provincial Park.

344. C. Duncan
The hockey stick is 62.5 metres long.

CANADIAN GEOGRAPHY WITH SOME ODDITIES THROWN IN FOR GOOD MEASURE

QUESTIONS 345 – 349

345. Yellowknife is on the northern shore of what lake?
A. Great Bear Lake
B. Great Slave Lake
C. Lake Winnipeg

346. What large enclosed bay forms the northwestern end of the harbour at Halifax?
A. Bedford Basin
B. Cootes Paradise
C. Burlington Bay

347. In what province would you find the Cabot Trail?
A. Newfoundland and Labrador
B. Nova Scotia
C. New Brunswick

348. In what province would you find Galiano Island?
A. Nova Scotia
B. Ontario
C. British Columbia

349. Which province is the site of the reconstructed French Jesuit settlement of Sainte-Marie Among the Hurons?
A. Québec
B. New Brunswick
C. Ontario

345. B. Great Slave Lake

It is the deepest lake in North America.

346. A. Bedford Basin

It is 8 kilometres long and 5 kilometres wide, and because of its sheltered locale, was the ideal, safe staging point for Atlantic convoys during both World Wars.

347. B. Nova Scotia

Cabot Trail is a 300-kilometre highway and scenic route that lops around the northern tip of Cape Breton Island.

348. C. British Columbia

Galiano Island is in the Strait of Georgia and is named after Spanish explorer Dionisio Alcala Galiano.

349. C. Ontario

The settlement is near Midland and the original settlement existed from 1639 to 1649.

CANADIAN GEOGRAPHY WITH SOME ODDITIES THROWN IN FOR GOOD MEASURE

QUESTIONS 350 – 353

350. What province is sometimes called the "Keystone Province"?

A. Ontario
B. Manitoba
C. Saskatchewan

351. What freshwater lake has the largest surface area in the world?

A. Lake Superior
B. Great Slave Lake
C. Great Bear Lake

352. What waterway links the Atlantic Ocean with the Great Lakes?

A. Rideau Canal
B. St. Lawrence Seaway
C. Malacca Straits

353. Which British Columbia lake is the supposed home of a Loch Ness–like sea monster named Ogopogo?

A. Mabel Lake
B. Chilko Lake
C. Okanagan Lake

Answers 350 – 353

350. B. Manitoba

"Keystone Province" is in reference to the province's role, or perhaps location, in uniting east to west.

351. A. Lake Superior

Some statisticians include the Caspian Sea as a lake, but many do not. For our purposes, we do not, which makes Lake Superior the world's largest lake by surface area, which just happens to be 82,414 km².

352. B. St. Lawrence Seaway

353. C. Okanagan Lake

The modern era for promoting the tourist attraction that Ogopogo has become began around 1926, though First Nations people claim something large and monstrous has been living in the lake for hundreds of years.

QUESTIONS 354–358

354. In what western Canadian province would you find the town Norway House?

A. Manitoba
B. Saskatchewan
C. Alberta

355. Which of the Great Lakes is considered to be the headwaters of the entire waterway?

A. Lake Nipigon
B. Lake Ontario
C. Lake Superior

356. What is Canada's longest river?

A. Fraser River
B. St. Lawrence River
C. Mackenzie River

357. What is the highest point in Ontario?

A. Blue Mountain
B. Tip Top Mountain
C. Ishpatina Ridge

358. On which New Brunswick river would you find the "reversing falls" rapids?

A. Saint John River
B. Miramichi River
C. Hammond River

Answers 354–358

354. A. Manitoba

Norway House was originally founded as a Hudson's Bay Trading Post in the 18th century. It shares its name with the Norway House Cree Nation Reserve and has both a chief and a mayor.

355. C. Lake Superior

Lake Nipigon is considered by some to be the sixth Great Lake, but not officially.

356. C. Mackenzie River

The river originates in Great Slave Lake and is 1738 kilometres long. With its headstreams, it is 4241 kilometres long, which makes it the second longest river in North America after the Mississippi-Missouri rivers.

357. C. Ishpatina Ridge

It is 90 kilometres north of Sudbury and has an elevation of 693 metres.

358. A. Saint John River

QUESTIONS 359 – 361

359. What lake, shared by Québec and New York State, is apparently home to a lake monster dubbed Champ?

A. Lac Memphrémagog
B. Lake Pohénégamook
C. Lake Champlain

360. What Ontario island is the largest freshwater island in the world?

A. Manitoulin Island
B. Pelee Island
C. Goat Island

361. Which Alberta town has a UFO landing pad?

A. Lethbridge
B. St. Paul
C. Drumheller

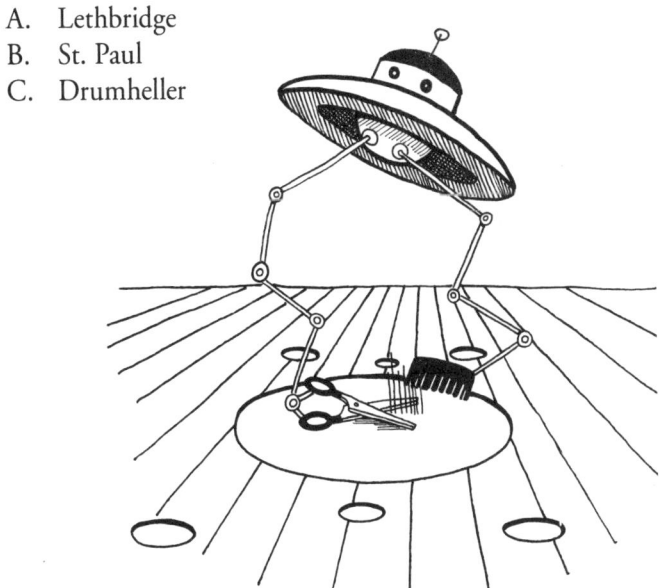

Answers 359 – 361

359. C. Lake Champlain

Lac Memphrémagog and Lake Pohénégamook both have lake monsters of their own, respectively called Memphré and Ponik.

360. A. Manitoulin Island

Manitoulin Island lies entirely within Lake Huron.

361. B. St. Paul

Built as a centennial project and officially opened in 1967, the UFO Landing Pad at St. Paul, Alberta, has been visited by notable dignitaries, including Mother Theresa and Queen Elizabeth II, though never officially by a UFO.

CANADIAN WILDLIFE, ENVIRONMENT AND WEATHER

Unique species, environmental concerns and, heck, what Canadians don't like to concern themselves with weather? Well, they're all here in this chapter of big teeth, big storms and big freezes. So after this winter of woe (2007–08), let's all dig in for some real Canadian questions of frost-bitten memories and cute and fuzzy creatures. Oh, and an amphibian and a pollinator are thrown in for good measure! And then there are the provincial flowers and birds as well.

362. What is the smallest dog-like animal native to Canada and has more young per litter than any wild mammal in the world?
  A. Red fox
  B. Arctic fox
  C. Wolverine

363. Which province has the lady's slipper as its floral emblem and lies north of Nova Scotia and east of New Brunswick?
  A. Prince Edward Island
  B. Québec
  C. Nova Scotia

364. Which Canadian capital city wins the title for having the most number of wet days in 2006?
  A. Charlottetown
  B. Victoria
  C. St. John's

362. B. Arctic fox

The arctic fox is also known as *Alopex lagopus* and measures between 75 and 115 centimetres in length. It also weighs anywhere from 2.5 to 9 kilograms. It has a long, bushy tail and a white or whitish coat in winter, whereas the coat is darker brown or grey in summer. The average litter of whelps is 11, which are born in May or early June. Litters of up to 22 have also been recorded.

363. A. Prince Edward Island

It gets its name from its petals that are shaped like a lady's shoe.

364. C. St. John's

In 2004, the top three wettest capital cities in Canada, according to the number of wet days, were St. John's (215.6 days), Charlottetown (184.2 days) and Québec City (181.9 days).

CANADIAN WILDLIFE, ENVIRONMENT AND WEATHER

Questions 365 – 368

365. Which territory has the mountain avens as its floral emblem and has the second largest area?

A. Nunavut
B. Northwest Territories
C. Yukon

366. Which province has the trillium as its floral emblem and is the second largest province in terms of area?

A. Québec
B. Manitoba
C. Ontario

367. What species is resident in Canada and is considered to be the largest land carnivore?

A. Cougar
B. Grizzly bear
C. Polar bear

368. Which of the following communities recorded the lowest average monthly temperature to date in Canada and North America?

A. Eureka, Nunavut
B. Beaver Creek, Yukon
C. Yellowknife, Northwest Territories

ANSWERS 365 – 368

365. B. Northwest Territories

366. C. Ontario

367. C. Polar bear

Polar bears can weigh up to 800 kilograms, but on average weigh between 400 and 600 kilograms. They usually measure up to 260 centimetres in length, which is the equivalent of 2.6 metres. At birth, polar bears weigh less one kilogram. They have translucent hair and black skin that helps them absorb and preserve body heat.

368. A. Eureka, Nunavut

The lowest average monthly temperature was –47.9°C, and it was recorded in February 1979, when Eureka was still part of the Northwest Territories. Eureka is on Ellesmere Island.

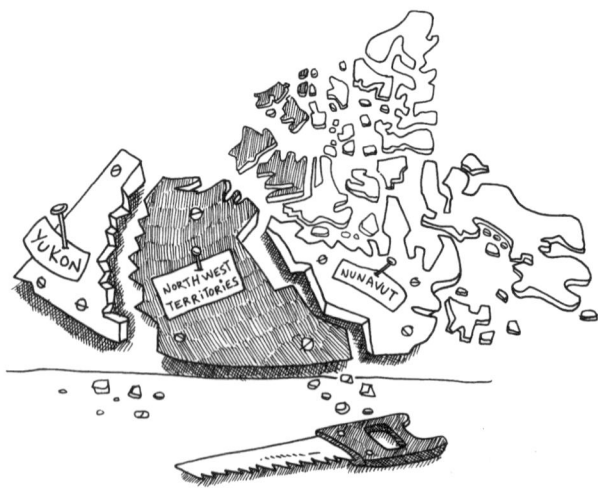

Questions 369–371

369. Which whale species found in the St. Lawrence is listed as threatened and has been officially protected by the Canadian Fisheries Act since 1979?

A. Killer whale
B. Beluga whale
C. Bowhead whale

370. Which of the following mammals lives in every province and territory in Canada?

A. Bat
B. Eastern grey squirrel
C. Snowshoe hare

371. Which province has the prairie crocus as its floral emblem and derives its name from a Cree word meaning "the place where the spirit speaks"?

A. Manitoba
B. Saskatchewan
C. Alberta

369. B. Beluga whale

Adult belugas have bulging foreheads and pure white skin. In Russian, "beluga" means "the white one," though newborns, calves and young belugas have brown or grey skin that eventually turns white. They weigh up to 1500 kilograms and average 3–5 metres in length. The St. Lawrence belugas are in the southernmost limits of the species range. Belugas as a species were hunted to excess between 1880 and 1950. Although they have been protected in the St. Lawrence since 1979, the species has not recovered in any noticeable numbers. That's probably because of pollution as well as increased traffic in the St. Lawrence.

370. C. Snowshoe hare

Officially known as *Lepus americanus,* the snowshoe hare is one of the most common forest dwellers in North America. It can leap up to 3 metres in a single bound, though Superman can still outdo him, and the little snowshoe can also travel up to 45 kilometres per hour.

371. A. Manitoba

In Cree, "Manitou" means "spirit."

CANADIAN WILDLIFE, ENVIRONMENT AND WEATHER

QUESTIONS 372–375

372. What is the largest rodent in North America and also a Canadian icon, though it has never been *Canadian Idol?*

A. Lemming
B. Beaver
C. Chipmunk

373. Which territory has the rock ptarmigan as its official bird and also encompasses one-fifth of the land in Canada?

A. Yukon
B. Northwest Territories
C. Nunavut

374. From which direction do the prevailing winds blow in Canada?

A. North
B. West
C. East

375. What familiar North American mammal has flexible lips as well as a very long tongue it manipulates to help it gather food such as ants and blueberries?

A. Swift fox
B. Mountain sheep
C. Black bear

372. B. Beaver

Officially known as *Castor canadensis,* the beaver is indeed the largest rodent in North America and only second in the world to South America's capybara. Adult beavers weigh from 15 to 32 kilograms, and a large adult can reach up to 1.3 metres in length (including a 30-centimetre tail). The beaver's Pleistocene-era ancestors were even larger, measuring up to 3 metres and weighing in at 350 kilograms. On land, beavers are rather slow and clumsy, though in the water they are graceful and extremely strong swimmers that can reach speeds near 7 kilometres per hour.

373. C. Nunavut

374. B. West

The prevailing winds are the trends in direction and speed of wind over a particular point on the Earth's surface.

375. C. Black bear

Officially called *Ursus americanus,* the black bear is quite common on the North American continent as far as wild animals go. Although they are often thought to be slow moving, black bears can reach speeds of 55–60 kilometres per hour. Adult males typically weigh 135 kilograms, though on rare occasions some black bears can grow to more than double that weight.

CANADIAN WILDLIFE, ENVIRONMENT AND WEATHER

QUESTIONS 376 – 378

376. Which province or territory has the common raven as its official bird and derives its name from a Native word meaning "greatest river"?

A. Yukon
B. Québec
C. Saskatchewan

377. What morning whistler is the largest thrush found in North America and has thrived in the face of human encroachment and climate change?

A. Blue jay
B. American robin
C. Bluebird

378. What North American mammal is known for revealing the white underside of its tail and accompanying white buttocks?

A. White-tailed deer
B. Caribou
C. Pale-buttocked streaker

376. A. Yukon

The Loucheux Indian word "Yuchoo" means the "greatest river" and refers to the Yukon River.

377. B. American robin

The American robin was named by early settlers who thought it looked like the English robin. Except for its red breast, the American robin doesn't really look much like the English robin, but then again, I guess the early settlers were more interested in settling than being scientifically accurate. Its breeding range stretches across North America. Unlike many species, the American robin has adapted quite well to habitat changes. Declining forests, increased farm sizes and the growth of cities has created larger breeding habitat for the robins.

378. A. White-tailed deer

Odocoileus virginianus (white-tailed deer) is one of the most widely distributed large animals in North America. It's found from the farthest southern tip of North America to as far north as Alaska and the Northwest Territories and Yukon. One of the more amusing accounts of "thinning of the herd" type of death for this species involves bucks fighting during mating season. On occasion, a pair of sparring bucks will get their antlers hopelessly tangled. The two bucks will slowly die if they can't disentangle their antlers.

Questions 379 – 381

379. In 2006 what was the snowiest capital city in Canada (in average annual snowfall)?

A. Charlottetown
B. Québec City
C. St. John's

380. Which province recently changed its floral emblem from the Madonna lily to the blue flag iris?

A. Québec
B. New Brunswick
C. Nova Scotia

381. In 2006, what was the coldest capital city in Canada (according to the average low temperature in the coldest month)?

A. Whitehorse
B. Yellowknife
C. Winnipeg

Answers 379 – 381

379. C. St. John's

The top five Canadian capital cities according to their average annual snowfall are:

- St. John's, 322.3 centimetres
- Québec City, 315.9 centimetres
- Charlottetown, 311.9 centimetres
- Fredericton, 276.5 centimetres
- Halifax, 230.5 centimetres

380. A. Québec

The Madonna lily was Québec's official flower for 36 years. It looks like the heraldic fleur-de-lis on Québec's flag. The Madonna lily is the symbol of French culture in France and Québec, but it does not grow naturally in the province. Therefore, in 1999, Québec chose a new flower that grows throughout the province: the blue flag iris.

381. B. Yellowknife

The top 10 coldest capital cities or major cities according to their average low temperature in their coldest month (which is January for all!) are:

- Yellowknife, –30.9°C
- Winnipeg, –22.8°C
- Whitehorse, –22°C
- Regina, –21.6°C
- Edmonton, –19.1°C
- Québec City, –17.6°C
- Fredericton, –15.5°C
- Ottawa, –15.3°C
- Calgary, –15.1°C
- Montréal, –14.7°C

CANADIAN WILDLIFE, ENVIRONMENT AND WEATHER

QUESTIONS 382 – 385

382. Which province or territory has the purple saxifrage as its floral emblem and encompasses Baffin Island?

   A. Northwest Territories
   B. Nunavut
   C. Newfoundland and Labrador

383. Which of the following communities recorded the lowest temperature in Canada to date?

   A. Alert, Nunavut
   B. Snag, Yukon
   C. Yellowknife, Northwest Territories

384. Which province has the great horned owl as its official bird and is also Canada's fourth largest province?

   A. Saskatchewan
   B. Alberta
   C. Manitoba

385. Which Fraser River fish species has seen a rapid decline since 1996 and may have lost as much as 60 percent of its kind?

   A. Coho salmon
   B. Large mouth bass
   C. Sturgeon

WHAT IS CANADA?

Answers 382–385

382. B. Nunavut

383. B. Snag, Yukon

The lowest temperature ever recorded in Canada and North America to date is −62.8°C on February 3, 1947. Snag is a few kilometres south of Beaver Creek, Yukon, not far from the Alaska border.

384. B. Alberta

385. A. Coho salmon

Although it has not yet been listed by the Species At Risk Act (SARA), the Interior Fraser River coho salmon has been listed as endangered by COSEWIC (Committee on the Status of Endangered Wildlife in Canada). COSEWIC is an independent committee of wildlife experts and scientists that was established in 1977 to identify species at risk. The Interior Fraser River coho salmon is threatened by shifting marine conditions and freshwater habitats that continue to deteriorate. The Department of Fisheries has collaborated with Aboriginal groups, the provincial government and industry to develop a draft recovery strategy. Whether this species will survive remains to be seen.

386. In 2006, what was the hottest capital or major city in Canada (according to the average high temperature in the hottest month, which is July)?

A. Québec City
B. Toronto
C. Ottawa

387. Which province has the Atlantic puffin as its official bird and was the first place to respond to the distress signal from the doomed ocean liner *Titanic?*

A. Nova Scotia
B. Prince Edward Island
C. Newfoundland and Labrador

388. What mouse-like rodent is the smallest mammal of the High Arctic and controls much of the rhythm of animal life there?

A. Lemming
B. Marten
C. Raccoon

386. B. Toronto

The top 10 Canadian capital cities and major cities according to their average high temperature in their hottest month were:
- Toronto, 26.8°C
- Ottawa, 26.5°C
- Montréal, 26.2°C
- Winnipeg, 25.8°C
- Regina, 25.7°C
- Fredericton, 25.6°C
- Québec City, 25.0°C
- Halifax, 23.6°C
- Charlottetown, 23.2°C
- Calgary, 22.9°C

387. C. Newfoundland and Labrador

388. A. Lemming

The lemming lives in treeless areas of northern Canada, and because it is an important food source for ermines, arctic foxes, snowy owls and other animals, it determines what happens with much of the animal life in the tundra. Lemmings are small enough that they do not freeze despite staying active throughout the arctic winter. Adults are about 150 millimetres in length, including a long tail that is roughly 15 percent of that length.

Questions 389–391

389. Which province was named for Queen Victoria's father and has the blue jay as its official bird?

A. Alberta
B. Ontario
C. Prince Edward Island

390. In 2006, what was the wettest capital or major city in Canada according to total precipitation?

A. St. John's
B. Halifax
C. Vancouver

391. Which province has the osprey as its official bird and is the second smallest province?

A. New Brunswick
B. Nova Scotia
C. Newfoundland and Labrador

389. C. Prince Edward Island

Queen Victoria's father was Prince Edward, Duke of Kent. He was the son of King George III and younger brother to the Prince Regent, who took over the throne when their father went insane. The Prince Regent, who later became George IV, had only one child who died before Victoria was born. Prince Edward died after catching pneumonia when Victoria was just eight months old. George IV died in 1830 and was succeeded by his brother William IV. William IV died in 1837 and Victoria succeeded him to the thrown.

390. A. St. John's

The top 10 Canadian capital cities or major cities according to their total precipitation in 2006 are:
- St. John's, 1513.7 millimetres
- Halifax, 1452.2 millimetres
- Québec City, 1230.3 millimetres
- Vancouver, 1199 millimetres
- Charlottetown, 1173.3 millimetres
- Fredericton, 1143.3 millimetres
- Montréal, 978.9 millimetres
- Ottawa, 943.5 millimetres
- Victoria, 883.3 millimetres
- Toronto, 792.7 millimetres

391. B. Nova Scotia

Canadian Wildlife, Environment and Weather

Questions 392–394

392. What native of the Canadian Prairies has been expanding its habitat since the beginning of the 20th century and is a surprisingly (to some) fast runner and as wily as expected?

A. Wolf
B. Red fox
C. Coyote

393. What is the most important group of pollinators, of which there are 800 species in Canada, and was also the subject of a 2007 feature-length film starring the voice of Jerry Seinfeld?

A. Mosquitoes
B. Bees
C. Hummingbirds

394. What species of reptile is found in Canada and many other places and is the largest living reptile?

A. Common garter snake
B. American crocodile
C. Leatherback seaturtle

392. C. Coyote

Increased urban conditions as well as competing wolf populations, which have continued to decline, have helped the coyote thrive and, in fact, increase its numbers since the early 1900s. Coyotes can reach speeds up to 65 kilometres per hour in a run. They were originally found on the Prairies in Canada. It's a controversial animal because it is as intelligent and playful as a domestic dog, but it is also a fine predator known for killing small farm animals. In some parts of Canada, coyotes are incorrectly referred to as "brush wolves." But wolves are larger and hunt in packs. Coyotes will hunt small prey as loners, but often defend large kills as packs.

393. B. Bees

Upwards of 80 percent of flowering plants depend on pollinators such as the bee to help them transfer their pollen from one plant to another, thus making possible the fertilization essential to fruit and seed production. This process was the subject of the 2007 animated film *Bee Movie,* which starred the voices of Jerry Seinfeld and Renée Zellweger. Bumble bees are probably the best-known bee species actually native to Canada. Other bees, such as honey bees, were brought to Canada from other countries. Dwindling numbers of bees as a result of habitat loss can have drastic consequences for food crops as well as other plants and wilderness areas.

394. C. Leatherback seaturtle

Much larger than all other marine turtles, leatherbacks can weigh more than 900 kilograms, and their leather-like upper shells can grow to 2 metres or more in length. These turtles have been known to dive to almost 1300 metres and often migrates across entire oceans. Unlike tortoises, leatherback seaturtles cannot retract their flippers or head.

CANADA'S MILITARY HISTORY

Canada has a long, illustrious military history—if you believe a country's military can be an illustrious measure of itself. As for me, I think military actions are for the most part the result of political failures. How many times did Britain and France officially go to war in order to settle the question of who would own North America? Four times is the official answer, though if you drop the American Revolution in the mix, it would be five, and well, there are any number of skirmishes, attacks and cross-border raids too numerous to count that should be counted as well. And what gives with the whole notion that one country should have dominion over an entire continent? I mean, wasn't it big enough for many? I think the answer is yes; however, that wasn't good enough for France and Britain, who also basically discounted any idea of the First Nations having claim over the continent.

But beyond that, Canadians have fought in any number of wars, sometimes defending Canada, sometimes sort of defending us and sometimes just getting into the mix. All of this doesn't have much to do with Canada's illustrious military history. Or does it? Either way, Canadian military-related questions follow. Enjoy, or experience them at will. FIRE IN THE HOLE!

395. Sometimes called the first of four French and Indian Wars, which war was fought in colonial North America between 1689 and 1697 and ended with the signing of the Treaty of Rijswijk?
   A. King William's War
   B. King James' War
   C. Louis XV's War

WHAT IS CANADA?

ANSWER 395

395. A. King William's War

396. In 1690, who led the French and their Native allies in successful attacks against Schenectady and Salmon Falls, but never managed to take the main target, Boston?
  A. Marquis de Montcalm
  B. Duke of Salisbury
  C. Count de Frontenac

397. Who led the British in capturing Port Royal, but failed to take Québec?
  A. Captain James Cook
  B. Sir William Phipps
  C. Edward Cornwallis

398. Queen Anne's War was the second conflict between Great Britain and France over the control of North America, and it was fought at roughly the same time as what European war?
  A. War of the Austrian Succession
  B. War of the Spanish Succession
  C. Wars of the Roses

399. What western Massachusetts town was the site of a devastating raid by French soldiers and their Native allies in February 1704?
  A. Boston
  B. Deerfield
  C. Fall River

396. C. Count de Frontenac

Frontenac was the governor of Canada at the time. The 1690 raids on Schenectady (New York), Salmon Falls (Rollinsford, New Hampshire), as well as (Casco, Maine) were great successes, though they failed to amount to much more than raids. After these raids, most of the war was a tit-for-tat affair.

397. B. Sir William Phipps

Despite the success of Phipps' capture of Port Royal, in the ensuring Peace Treaty, Acadia was returned to France.

398. B. War of the Spanish Succession

The war was the result of Spain's Charles II dying childless. England, the Dutch Republic and France all laid claim to the Spanish throne and the ensuring war broke out.

399. B. Deerfield

Deerfield was a remote frontier town at the time. On February 29, 1704, several hundred French soldiers and their Native allies surprised and overran the town. During the battle (or massacre as Americans refer to it), 56 settlers were killed, including women and children. More than 100 survivors of the raid were then forced to march back to New France. Almost one quarter of the captives died on the march. The others were held as hostages, some for two and a half years. By 1706, 60 of them had been returned. However, 30 or more decided to stay in Canada among the inhabitants of New France or with the various First Nations tribes.

400. In 1710, who led the British in capturing Port Royal once again?
   A. Francis Nicholson
   B. George Washington
   C. Daniel Subercase

401. What was Port Royal renamed when it came under British control?
   A. Port-O-Royal
   B. Royal Port
   C. Annapolis Royal

402. What treaty ended Britain's part in Queen Anne's War?
   A. Treaty of Paris
   B. Treaty of Utrecht
   C. Treaty of Edinburgh

403. Which of the following did France cede to Britain at the end of Queen Anne's War?
   A. Newfoundland
   B. Acadia
   C. Rupert's Land

400. A. Francis Nicholson

Nicholson was 55 years old at the time. He was aided in his campaign by an Edinburgh soldier, Colonel Samuel Vetch, and Sir Charles Hobby, who was born in Boston but had been knighted by Queen Anne in 1705 "for his brave conduct in Jamaica at the time of the earthquake in 1692." The French commander, Daniel d'Auger de Subercase, and his garrison of 150 men were outnumbered and outgunned. The British had more than 3000 soldiers, of which at least 400 were regular "lobsterbacks."

401. C. Annapolis Royal

It was renamed in honour of Britain's monarch, Queen Anne.

402. B. Treaty of Utrecht

403. A, B and C

All are correct (though the treaty may have referred to "Rupert's Land" as the "Hudson Bay territory"). In the treaty, France ceded all of them to Britain, as well as the island of St. Kitts. France also recognized Queen Anne as the British sovereign and agreed to stop supporting James Edward, the son of the deposed king James II. In return, Louis XIV's grandson was recognized as the King of Spain, the first Bourbon king of that country. He was called Philip V.

Questions 404–407

404. What was the name of the North American phase (1744–48) of the War of the Austrian Succession?
A. King George's War
B. Seven Years' War
C. Wars of the Roses

405. What Cape Breton fort was captured by New Englanders on June 15, 1745?
A. Cherbourg
B. Port Royal
C. Louisburg

406. What treaty ended the War of the Austrian Succession?
A. Treaty of Utrecht (2)
B. Peace of Aix-la-Chapelle
C. Treaty of Paris

407. The French and Indian Wars (1754–63) was the North American theatre of what European war?
A. War of Jenkin's Ear
B. Seven Years' War
C. American Revolution

404. A. King George's War

The War of the Austrian Succession lasted from 1740 to 1748 and was precipitated by the death of the Charles VI, Holy Roman Emperor and head of Austria's house of Hapsburg. Britain supported Maria Theresa's claim to the Austrian throne. France unsuccessfully supported the claim of Charles Albert, elector of Bavaria to the Imperial Hapsburg crown. However, much of the conflict had more to do with the fight between Britain and France over colonial claims in North America and India.

405. C. Louisburg

The fort's name was later changed to Louisbourg, named for Louis XIV. Louisburg became an important fishing and shipbuilding centre. Sir William Pepperell and a force of New Englanders with the support of the British Navy attacked the fort. After 48 days under siege, the garrison finally surrendered.

406. B. Peace of Aix-la-Chapelle

The treaty saw Britain and France basically return to where they were when the conflict first began. The fate of North America remained to be settled.

407. B. Seven Years' War

Often considered a World War, the Seven Years' War actually lasted nine years in North America. The War of Jenkins' Ear began in 1739 and was fought between Britain and Spain. It eventually merged into the War of the Austrian Succession. The "Jenkins' Ear" in question involved Captain Robert Jenkins, who appeared before the British Parliament waving his severed ear, which he said had been cut off by the Spanish in the West Indies.

408. Who was the commander of British forces at the decisive Battle of Québec on September 13, 1759?
A. James Wolfe
B. Marquis de Montcalm
C. Edward Cornwallis

409. Who commanded French forces at the Battle of Québec on September 13, 1759?
A. Marquis de Montcalm
B. Comte de Frontenac
C. General Papineau

410. What future explorer made the British victory at Québec possible by charting a way for British ships past hazards in the St. Lawrence River?
A. George Washington
B. George Vancouver
C. James Cook

411. What treaty ended the Seven Years' War (and the French and Indian Wars) and saw Britain awarded control over North America?
A. Treaty of Utrecht
B. Treaty of Paris
C. Treaty of Québec

ANSWERS 408 – 411

408. A. (Major General) James Wolfe

409. A. Marquis de Montcalm

410. C. James Cook
The French had removed markers in the river that had guided larger ships past shallow waters and rapids. When Wolfe's ships arrived at Québec, James Cook was given the task of charting a safe passage for the large British ships and troop carriers. Cook ventured into the St. Lawrence at night in a small boat with a few men and in the end got the job done. Without his amazing skills as a navigator, the Battle of Québec might not have taken place.

411. B. Treaty of Paris
The treaty was signed in Paris on February 10, 1763.

QUESTIONS 412 – 415

412. What Canadian city was abandoned by Sir Guy Carleton and the British in October 1775?
A. Québec City
B. Montréal
C. Halifax

413. What Canadian city was attacked during a snowstorm by American colonials led by Richard Montgomery and Benedict Arnold on December 31, 1775?
A. Halifax
B. Annapolis Royal
C. Québec City

414. What New Brunswick fort was attacked by New England rebels in November 1776?
A. Fort Cumberland
B. Louisbourg
C. Annapolis Royal

415. During the War of 1812, what French Canadian militia unit were the heroes of the Battle of Châteauguay?
A. The Royal 22e Regiment
B. The Voltigeurs
C. The Winnipeg Rifles

Answers 412 – 415

412. B. Montréal

Under Carleton's leadership, Montréal was abandoned after American forces had already taken Ticonderoga, Crown Point, Fort Chambly and Fort Saint-Jean.

413. C. Québec City

The American attack was repulsed and General Montgomery was killed. The American colonials kept up the siege of Québec until May 1776 when they finally abandoned the campaign.

414. A. Fort Cumberland

Lieutenant-Colonel Joseph Goreham and his troops easily foiled the attack. The fort was originally built by the French and called Fort Beausejour. It is located near present-day Sackville, New Brunswick.

415. B. The Voltigeurs

The original corps of Voltigeurs was disbanded in 1815; however, a regiment in today's Canadian Forces still bears its name.

QUESTIONS 416 – 419

416. What army officer and protégé of the Duke of Kent was responsible for recruiting the Voltigeurs Canadiens?
   A. Charles de Salaberry
   B. Sir Isaac Brock
   C. John Graves Simcoe

417. At the 1885 Battle of Duck Lake, who was the military commander of the Métis?
   A. Louis Riel
   B. Sam Steele
   C. Gabriel Dumont

418. Who commanded Canadian government troops at the Battle of Batoche in May 1885?
   A. Sam Steele
   B. Lief Crozier
   C. Frederick Middleton

419. In what country did Canadians distinguish themselves at the Battle of Paardeberg?
   A. South Africa
   B. India
   C. Ireland

416. A. Charles de Salaberry

He was born in Beauport, Québec, in 1778 and started to serve in the British Army in 1794. He served in Ireland, the West Indies and in the Low Countries during the wars with Napoleon.

417. C. Gabriel Dumont

More of an enlarged scuffle than a battle, the Battle of Duck Lake began on March 26, 1885. During a negotiation, a Cree emissary and a police interpreter disagreed. It then got out of hand, and after about a half hour of skirmishes, the North-West Mounted Police and their volunteers retreated. They lost 12 out of a force of about 100. Six of the rebels died, including Gabriel Dumont's brother, Isidore. Gabriel himself was wounded.

418. C. (Major General) Frederick Middleton

Middleton was sent west after the Battle of Duck Lake and put in charge of about 5000 men. Most of the force was made up of Ontario militia units, though there were also two Québec battalions and one from Nova Scotia. The West also contributed about 1700 men. Superintendent Lief Crozier was the man in charge of the NWMP and its volunteers at Duck Lake. Superintendent Sam Steele was in charge of a force that saw the last shots fired during the rebellion, which took place at Loon Lake on June 3 1885. None of Steele's men were lost, but four Cree died.

419. A. South Africa

QUESTIONS 420–423

420. What war lasted from 1899 to 1902 between the British Empire (including Canada) and two Afrikaner republics?
   A. Crimean War
   B. Boer War
   C. Spanish-American War

421. What treaty was signed in 1902 that ended the Boer War?
   A. Treaty of Paris
   B. Treaty of London
   C. Peace of Vereeniging

422. In what city was the Peace Treaty ending the Boer War signed?
   A. Pretoria
   B. Johannesburg
   C. Cape Town

423. Who was the first Canadian-appointed commander of the Canadian Corps during World War I?
   A. Sir Arthur Currie
   B. Andrew McNaughton
   C. Sir Sam Hughes

ANSWERS 420 – 423

420. B. Boer War

It was also known as the Second Boer War, or the South African War. Two Boer republics opposed Great Britain in the Boer War. They were Orange Free State and Transvaal (or the South African Republic).

421. C. Peace of Vereeniging

422. A. Pretoria

423. A. Sir Arthur Currie

He took control of Canadian troops in 1917; before that they were led by British commanders.

Questions 424–427

424. At what April 1915 battle were Canadians subjected to the first effective gas attack on the Western Front?

A. Ypres
B. Cambrai
C. Mont Sorrel

425. In 1917, what World War I battle was fought over Easter weekend in northern France?

A. Paschendale
B. Juttland
C. Vimy Ridge

426. What Canadian World War I ace won the most aerial victories in Commonwealth history?

A. Billy Bishop
B. Roy Brown
C. Raymond Collishaw

427. What Canadian-born flying ace was credited with shooting down the Red Baron?

A. Billy Bishop
B. Roy Brown
C. Raymond Collishaw

Answers 424 – 427

424. A. Ypres

As a result of the gas attack, a wide gap opened in the allied lines, which was quickly filled by the First Canadian Division together with other British troops.

425. C. Vimy Ridge

It was finally won by Canadian troops in April 1917.

426. A. Billy Bishop

He had 72 aerial victories.

427. B. Roy Brown

He was officially credited with shooting down and killing Manfred von Richtofen, but it is just as likely that the Red Baron was felled by ground fire from Australian machine guns. Nonetheless, Brown was a distinguished flyer and is credited with 11 victories.

428. In 1917, what Canadian city suffered the world's largest non-nuclear explosion when two ships collided in its harbour?
   A. St. John's
   B. Halifax
   C. Québec City

429. Canada's Mackenzie-Papineau Battalion fought in the civil war of what country?
   A. Portugal
   B. Spain
   C. China

430. What Montréal-born doctor served in the Spanish Civil War and became a hero in China?
   A. Frederick Banting
   B. Wilder Penfield
   C. Norman Bethune

431. From 1939 to December 1943, who commanded Canada's forces in Britain?
   A. G.G. Simonds
   B. Harry Crerar
   C. Andrew McNaughton

428. B. Halifax

On December 6, 1917, two ships, *Mont Blanc* (a French munitions ship heavily laden with explosives) and *Imo* (a Belgian relief ship, empty at the time), collided in the narrows leading to Halifax's inner harbour, the Bedford Basin. The Belgian ship was in the wrong place and thwarting the rules of the sea (by passing to right). *Imo* struck *Mont Blanc,* missing the hold containing TNT, but striking a hold containing benzol fuel and unstable picric acid. The collision caused sparks to fly from the two steel vessels and a fire began on *Mont Blanc.* The fire quickly spread and was out of control, forcing the French crew to abandon ship and row for the Dartmouth shore. *Mont Blanc* drifted to Pier 6 and soon the fire spread there. At 9:04 AM *Mont Blanc* exploded. For two square miles around Pier 6 nothing was left standing. More than 1500 people died instantly. In the end, 1900 people died and 6000 were left without shelter.

429. B. Spain

It was a Canadian battalion of volunteers.

430. C. Norman Bethune

431. C. Andrew McNaughton

QUESTIONS 432 – 435

432. On what date did Canada declare war on Germany in 1939?
A. September 1
B. September 10
C. September 3

433. Who opened the Sarajevo airport for humanitarian aid during the height of the Bosnian war when he created and commanded Sector Sarajevo as part of the United Nations protection force in May 1992?
A. Lewis MacKenzie
B. Romeo Daillaire
C. Rick Hillier

434. On Christmas Day 1941, the Royal Rifles of Canada and the Winnipeg Grenadiers surrendered to Japan in what battle?
A. Battle of Hong Kong
B. Battle of the Philippines
C. Pearl Harbor

435. Canadians fought in what 1940 World War II battle that took place entirely in the air?
A. Battle of Britain
B. Battle of the Atlantic
C. Battle of France

Answers 432–435

432. B. September 10

On September 1, 1939, Germany invaded Poland. Poland then pleaded with its allies, Great Britain and France, for assistance. Great Britain presented an ultimatum to Germany on September 3, which said that unless Germany withdrew its troops from Poland within two hours, a state of war would exist between the British Empire and Germany. Germany did not comply, and on September 3, 1939, the British Empire was officially at war with Germany. Australia, New Zealand, India and France declared war on Germany on that same day. South Africa declared war on Germany on September 6. Canada declared war on Germany on September 10, 1939. The Soviet Union acted upon its August agreement with Germany and attacked Poland on September 17. Finally, on October 6, 1939, Poland was defeated.

433. A. Lewis MacKenzie

As part of the UN protection force in the former Yugoslavia, Major General Lewis MacKenzie created Sector Sarajevo and with a contingent of soldiers from 31 countries managed to get the Sarajevo airport opened to receive humanitarian aid. Since then, MacKenzie has been an outspoken commentator and critic of governments and military actions throughout the world.

434. A. Battle of Hong Kong

435. A. Battle of Britain

436. In which country did Canadians fight the Battle of Kapyong in 1951?
A. China
B. Korea
C. Vietnam

437. Lester B. Pearson was awarded the 1957 Nobel Peace Prize for his part in helping to settle what 1956 crisis?
A. Cyprus Crisis
B. Suez Crisis
C. Cuban Missile Crisis

438. In what northern French seaport did the Second Canadian Infantry Division suffer serious losses in August 1942?
A. Calais
B. Cherbourge
C. Dieppe

439. In what country were Canadian troops deployed near Kandahar in 2002?
A. Afghanistan
B. Somalia
C. Iraq

440. What is the highest position one can attain in the Canadian military?
A. Minister of Defence
B. Chief of Defence Staff
C. Vice Admiral

Answers 436–440

436. B. Korea

437. B. Suez Crisis
After Egypt's Nasser nationalized the Suez Canal, Britain, France and Israel attacked and took the canal back by force. Pearson's invention and legacy emerging from the crisis was in creating the concept of the United Nations Emergency Force (UNEF), or peacekeepers who were sent in to keep the borders at peace while a political solution was being worked out.

438. C. Dieppe

439. A. Afghanistan

440. B. Chief of Defence Staff

AMATEUR AND OLYMPIC SPORTS

These are the sports that I think everyone really loves. It has a lot to do with doing something just for the sake of giving it your all—pulling out all the stops to reach the top of your game. I think most of us admire non-professional athletes because they play sports for the sheer competition, not for financial or personal gain (for the most part), and also because these elite competitors constantly do what most of us don't—test their limits.

There's also something about national pride that kicks in at international sporting events and especially at the Olympics, where we hold our own against the biggest nations in the world. Some of these behemoth nations have 10 times our population, money and resources to pull from. That makes our own resources seem puny by comparison. And yet still the underdog wins. Who doesn't love a come-from-behind story? We live in the shadow of a huge and mostly affable neighbour, but when we beat Americans at a game, sport or competition, we absolutely love it! We are so small next to them and are rather docile for the most part, but on occasion Canadians beat the pants off Americans, and it feels really good.

This chapter is a celebration of all those athletes who compete their little hearts out, humble us all and make us proud!

(Note: All the Olympic records and standings listed here do not include the 2008 Beijing Olympics, since I'm writing all of this before these games have taken place.)

441. At the opening ceremonies of the 2002 Olympic winter games, who carried the Canadian flag?
A. Annie Perreault
B. Catriona Le May Doan
C. Jennifer Botterill

Answer 441

441. B. Catriona Le May Doan

Speed skater Le May Doan had earlier won gold in the 500 metres and bronze in the 1000 metres at the 1998 Nagano Olympics. At the 2002 Olympics in Salt Lake City, she again took the gold in the 500 metres.

AMATEUR AND OLYMPIC SPORTS

QUESTIONS 442–445

442. What 1993 film starred John Candy and is about a Jamaican bobsled team?
   A. *Bob Marley and the Wailers*
   B. *Wagons East*
   C. *Cool Runnings*

443. The Jamaican bobsled team made their first appearance during what city's 1988 Winter Olympics?
   A. Vancouver
   B. Calgary
   C. Montréal

444. At the 2000 Summer Olympics in Sydney, what duo won the gold medal for Men's Doubles in tennis?
   A. Sébastien Lareau and Daniel Nestor
   B. Todd Woodbridge and Mark Woodforde
   C. Alex Corretja and Albert Costa

445. Who was the skip of Canada's gold medal–winning female curling team at the 1998 Winter Olympics in Nagano, Japan?
   A. Jan Betker
   B. Joan McCusker
   C. Sandra Schmirler

Answers 442 – 445

442. C. *Cool Runnings*

443. B. Calgary

444. A. Sébastien Lareau and Daniel Nestor
Lareau, born in Montréal, and Nestor, who was born in Belgrade in the former Yugoslavia, took the gold for Canada, beating Americans Todd Woodbridge and Mark Woodforde. Spain's Alex Corretja and Albert Costa took the bronze medal.

445. C. Sandra Schmirler
Schmirler's teammates were Jan Betker, Atina Ford, Marcia Gudereit and Joan McCusker. The silver medal went to the team from Denmark and the bronze to Sweden. In 1999, Schmirler was diagnosed with esophageal cancer. She succumbed to it on March 3, 2000, at age 36. More than 15,000 people attended her funeral, which was broadcast nationwide.

QUESTIONS 446 – 449

446. Which *two* female rowers were the first Canadians to win three Olympic gold medals?
A. Silken Laumann
B. Marnie McBean
C. Kathleen Heddle

447. In 1960, who won Canada's first-ever Olympic gold medal in skiing?
A. Nancy Greene
B. Kathy Kreiner
C. Anne Heggtveit

448. At the Winter Olympics in 2002, who did Canada defeat to take the gold in women's hockey?
A. United States
B. Norway
C. Sweden

449. In what city were the 1976 Summer Olympic Games held?
A. Los Angeles
B. Calgary
C. Montréal

Answers 446 – 449

446. B. Marnie McBean, and C. Kathleen Heddle

Together they won gold in the coxless pairs at the Barcelona games, and with Jennifer Barnes, Shannon Crawford, Megan Delehanty, Jessica Monroe, Brenda Taylor, Lesley Thompson and Kay Worthington, they won gold in the coxed eight. At the Atlanta games in 1996, McBean and Heddle won gold in the double sculls, and with Laryssa Biesenthal and Diane O'Grady, they won the bronze in quadruple sculls.

447. C. Anne Heggtveit

At the Squaw Valley Olympics in 1962, Heggtveit took the gold medal in the women's slalom. American Betsy Snite took the silver, and Barbara Henneberger of the combined German team took the bronze. Squaw Valley is in California for those too young to remember.

448. A. United States

The Canadian women's team beat the Americans 3–2; Sweden won the bronze medal.

449. C. Montréal

AMATEUR AND OLYMPIC SPORTS

Questions 450–453

450. In the 1976 Olympic Summer games, what Canadian athlete won a silver medal in the high jump?

A. Greg Joy
B. John Wood
C. Clay Evans

451. What Canadian swimmer set an Olympic record in the backstroke on his way to a gold medal at the 1992 Barcelona Olympics?

A. Marcel Grey
B. Mark Tewksbury
C. Stephen Clarke

452. Who was crowned the "fastest man in the world" at the 1996 Atlanta Olympics when he ran the 100-metre race in 9.84 seconds?

A. Robert Esmie
B. Bruny Surin
C. Donovan Bailey

453. Which country won the gold medal in the men's 4x100-metre relay at the 1996 Atlanta Olympics?

A. Canada
B. Brazil
C. United States

450. A. Greg Joy

For the first time in Summer Olympics history, the host nation (that's right, Canada) failed to win a gold medal. Canada, however, won five silver medals, including one won by Greg Joy in the high jump. Jacek Wszola of Poland won the gold in the high jump, and Dwight Stones of the United States took the bronze. The minuscule measure of 0.02 metres separated both gold from silver, and silver from bronze.

451. B. Mark Tewksbury

Tewksbury beat Americans Jeff Rouse and David Berkoff, who took the silver and gold medals, respectively. As well, Tewksbury, together with Stephen Clarke, Jonathan Cleveland and Marcel Grey, won a bronze medal for Canada in the men's 4x100-metre medley.

452. C. Donovan Bailey

Bailey beat Frankie Fredericks of Namibia, who took the silver medal, and Ato Boldon of Trinidad and Tobago, who took the bronze.

453. A. Canada

The Canadian relay team was made up of Donovan Bailey (who also won gold in the 100 metres), Robert Esmie, Bruny Surin and Glenroy Gilbert. The Canadians beat the Americans, who took the silver medal; the Brazilians took the bronze.

AMATEUR AND OLYMPIC SPORTS

QUESTIONS 454–457

454. At which Olympic Games did Canada win its first gold medal in ice hockey?

A. Antwerp (1920)
B. Chomonix (1924)
C. St. Moritz (1948)

455. In April 2004, the Canadian women's hockey team won their eighth world championship after defeating what country?

A. United States
B. Sweden
C. Russia

456. What *two* cities did Vancouver beat out in its successful final round bid for the 2010 Winter Olympic Games?

A. Munich, Germany
B. Salzburg, Austria
C. Pyeongchang, South Korea

457. In what sport did Percy Williams win the 100 metres and 200 metres for Canada at the 1928 Summer Olympics in Amsterdam?

A. Rowing
B. Swimming
C. Sprinting

WHAT IS CANADA?

Answers 454–457

454. A. Antwerp (1920)

The Antwerp Olympics were the first Winter Sports added to the Summer Games. There was no separate Winter Olympics at the time. Canada was represented in hockey by the Winnipeg Falcons. Canada beat Sweden 12–1 to take the gold medal; however, a rather complicated tournament meant that Sweden did not take the silver medal. In fact, the United States took silver, and Czechoslovakia took the bronze medal. The Canadian Olympic hockey team consisted of only eight men: Robert Benson, Walter Byron, Frank Fredrickson, Chris Fridfinnson, Magnus Goodman, Haldor Halderson, Konrad Johannesson and Allan Woodman.

455. A. United States

456. B. Salzburg, Austria, and C. Pyeongchang, South Korea

457. C. Sprinting

In the 100 metres, Percy Williams beat Jack London of Great Britain, who took the silver medal, and Georg Lammers of Germany who took the bronze. In the 200 metres, Williams beat Walter Rangeley of Great Britain who took the silver medal and Helmut Körnig of Germany who took the bronze.

AMATEUR AND OLYMPIC SPORTS

QUESTIONS 458–460

458. What sport is descended from the Ojibwa word "baag'adowe"?
  A. Field hockey
  B. Rounders
  C. Lacrosse

459. In what sport was Elvis Stojko a three-time world champion?
  A. Wrestling
  B. Figure skating
  C. Ice dancing

460. What trophy is awarded yearly to Canada's outstanding athlete?
  A. Jack Diamond Trophy
  B. Kraft Singles Trophy
  C. Lou Marsh Trophy

458. C. Lacrosse

The Ojibwa word literally means "bump hips." Other First Nation tribes had similar games by different names. Some of those names were "dehuntshigwa'es," which in Onondaga means "men hit a rounded object," and "tewaaarathon" in the Mohawk language, which means "little brother of war."

459. B. Figure skating

Stojko was Men's World Champion in Figure Skating in 1994, 1995 and 1997. He is a seven-time Canadian Figure Skating champion and a two-time silver medalist in the Olympics (1994, 1998).

460. C. Lou Marsh Trophy

First awarded in 1936, the award and trophy is named in honour of Lou Marsh, who over his career was variously an elite athlete, referee and sports editor at the *Toronto Star* newspaper. A panel of journalists vote for the top athlete, professional or amateur. The trophy has been awarded 68 times since 1936 (not awarded from 1942–44, because of World War II). Wayne Gretzky has won the Lou Marsh more than any other athlete (four times in all). Barbara Anne Scott is the top Lou Marsh winner for women, winning it three times.

Questions 461 – 462

461. In what sport did Silken Laumann become World Champion in 1991?

A. Swimming
B. Diving
C. Rowing

462. In what sport did the pair of Ian Millar and Big Ben compete from 1984 to 1994?

A. Equestrian
B. Fencing
C. Synchronized swimming

461. C. Rowing (single sculls)

Laumann also won the Lou Marsh Trophy and was named Canada's Athlete of the Year in 1991. However, her most amazing achievements (though perhaps not because she finished first) were still to come. She was a silver medalist at the 1996 Atlantic Olympics in the single sculls and previously won bronze for the same event in Barcelona in 1992. She also won a bronze medal with her sister Daniele in the double sculls at the 1984 Los Angeles Olympics. Laumann was a favourite to win gold at the 1992 Olympics until the boat of a pairs team collided with her during training in Germany in mid-May 1992. Five operations on her leg and three weeks in the hospital put a dent in her training schedule, but by late June she was back on the water. Despite the injuries and pain, she still managed to win the bronze medal in the single sculls.

462. A. Equestrian

At 17.3 hands high, Big Ben fit his name. He was the horse part of the horse and rider equestrian team. Big Ben was born in April 1976 in Belgium and was originally named "Winston," after Winston Churchill. Big Ben and Ian Millar began competing together in 1984. Big Ben won more than 40 Grand Prix titles, six of which were Spruce Meadows Derbys. He was also the World Cup Show Jumping Champion two years in a row (1988 and 1989). At the Olympics (in 1984 and 1988), Big Ben was part of two fourth-place teams. Big Ben retired in 1994 to the Millar's farm in Perth, Ontario. He is one of only two horses inducted into the Canadian Sports Hall of Fame (Northern Dancer is the other). He died at age 23 on December 11, 1999. In 2005 a bronze statue was erected in Perth, showing Ian Millar atop Big Ben in mid-jump.

AMATEUR AND OLYMPIC SPORTS

QUESTIONS 463 – 466

463. For what sport did Sylvie Frechette win a gold medal at the 1992 Barcelona Olympic games?

A. 100-metre butterfly
B. Fencing
C. Synchronized swimming

464. In what team sport did Haley Wickenheiser compete and win gold medals at both the Salt Lake City and Torino Olympic games?

A. Ice hockey
B. Basketball
C. Water polo

465. When was the last time the summer and winter Olympic games took place in the same year?

A. 1976
B. 1988
C. 1998

466. Which women's basketball team holds the North American record for best winning percentage of all time?

A. Hamilton Hoops
B. Edmonton Grads
C. Winnipeg Wheat Sheafs

ANSWERS 463 – 466

463. C. Synchronized swimming

More specifically, Frechette won the solo event of synchronized swimming. She actually shared the gold with American Kristen Babb-Sprague. Fumiko Okuno of Japan won the bronze medal. (This event has always been a bit of a loss to me. I understand how more than one swimmer can synchronize with others, but who do you synchronize with in the solo event? God or perhaps Neptune, I guess.)

464. A. Ice hockey

Wickenheiser also became the first woman to play professional hockey at a position other than goalie when she played for HC Salamat in Finland in 2003. That same year, she was the first woman to score a goal playing in a men's professional league.

465. B. 1988

That year, the Summer Olympics were held in Seoul, South Korea, and the Winter Olympics were held in Calgary.

466. B. Edmonton Grads

From 1915 to 1940, they won 502 games and lost only 20, giving them an incredible winning percentage of 96. They were disbanded in 1940 because of World War II.

AMATEUR AND OLYMPIC SPORTS

QUESTIONS 467 – 470

467. In 1988, who became the first person to swim across all five Great Lakes?
   A. Beth Whittall
   B. Florence Chadwick
   C. Vicki Keith

468. During Montréal's 1976 Summer Olympics, who became the first gymnast to score a perfect 10?
   A. Olga Korbut
   B. Dominique Dawes
   C. Nadia Comaneci

469. Which of the following Canadian athletes was stripped of a gold medal at the 1988 Seoul Summer Olympics?
   A. Guy Greavette
   B. Ben Johnson
   C. Geneviève Jeanson

470. In what decade was Canada's first curling Brier held?
   A. 1910s
   B. 1920s
   C. 1930s

Answers 467 – 470

467. C. Vicki Keith

She swam across all five Great Lakes over a two-month period in 1988. Keith is also the only person to complete the 104-kilometre double crossing of Lake Ontario. She continues to hold 16 world records.

468. C. Nadia Comaneci

She was awarded a perfect 10 score for her performance on the uneven bars. She went on to earn six additional 10s in the process of winning gold in the all-around, balance beam and uneven bars, as well as a bronze on the floor exercise and a silver with her Romanian teammates in the team competition.

469. B. Ben Johnson

He won the 100 metres at the Seoul Summer Olympics but was quickly stripped of the medal when a drug test determined he had been using performance-enhancing drugs.

470. B. 1920s

The first Brier took place in 1925, in Winnipeg to be exact, with the help of a man named George Cameron who had thoughts (or perhaps delusions of grandeur) of uniting Canada through curling. He convinced some sponsors, and before you knew it, the MacDonald-Brier Trophy appeared at the 1925 Manitoba Bonspiel. It's hard to believe, but it wasn't until the 1950s that the first world curling championships evolved.

AMATEUR AND OLYMPIC SPORTS

Questions 471–475

471. In 1930, which Ontario city was the site of the first British Empire Games?

A. Hamilton
B. Toronto
C. Ottawa

472. In 1999, what western Canadian city hosted the Pan-American Games?

A. Regina
B. Brandon
C. Winnipeg

473. How many times have Canadians won the gold medal in Olympic ice hockey?

A. 15
B. 11
C. 9

474. What trophy is awarded to the champions of the Canadian Hockey League?

A. Calder Cup
B. Emerald Cup
C. Memorial Cup

475. Which Canadian woman was the first person to swim across Lake Ontario?

A. Beth Whittall
B. Marilyn Bell
C. Vicki Keith

471. A. Hamilton

The name was later changed to the British Empire and Commonwealth Games and then to the British Commonwealth Games and finally to the Commonwealth Games.

472. C. Winnipeg

473. C. 9

Canadian men have won Olympic gold seven times (1920, 1924, 1928, 1932, 1948, 1952, 2002), and Canadian women have won twice (2002 and 2006).

474. C. Memorial Cup

It's the top prize in North America for men's junior (under 21) ice hockey.

475. B. Marilyn Bell

She was 16 years old at the time (September 1954) and swam the 52 kilometres in 20 hours and 59 minutes. She later went on to become the youngest person to swim the English Channel (in 1955).

Amateur and Olympic Sports

Questions 476 – 477

476. Which Summer Olympics provided Canada with its best medal count to date?
A. Athens, 2004
B. Los Angeles, 1984
C. Atlanta, 1996

477. Who currently holds the Olympic record in the men's 100 metres?
A. Donovan Bailey
B. Bruny Surin
C. Glenroy Gilbert

476. B. Los Angeles, 1984

The most successful Olympic summer games for Canada are as follows:

- Los Angeles, 1984, 44 medals (10 gold, 18 silver, 16 bronze)
- Atlanta, 1996, 22 medals (3 gold, 11 silver, 8 bronze)
- Barcelona, 1992, 18 medals (7 gold, 4 silver, 7 bronze)
- Amsterdam, 1928, 15 medals (4 gold, 4 silver, 7 bronze)
- Sydney, 2000, 14 medals (3 gold, 3 silver, 8 bronze)
- Los Angeles, 1932, 14 medals (2 gold, 5 silver, 7 bronze)
- London, England, 1908, 13 medals (3 gold, 3 silver, 7 bronze)
- Athens, 2004, 12 medals (3 gold, 6 silver, 3 bronze)
- Montréal, 1976, 11 medals (0 gold, 5 silver, 6 bronze)
- Seoul, 1988, 10 medals (3 gold, 2 silver, 5 bronze)

477. A. Donovan Bailey

His Olympic record still holds, though the time has been broken on the world stage. The world record for the 100 metres is currently held by Asafa Powell of Jamaica and is 9.74 seconds. Donovan Bailey's Olympic record will probably be beaten during the 2008 Beijing Olympics. For now, though, here are the top Olympians in the 100 metres:

- Donovan Bailey, Canada, 9.84s, Atlanta, 1996
- Carl Lewis, USA, 9.92s, Seoul, 1988
- Jim Hines, USA, 9.95s, Mexico City, 1968
- Bob Hayes, USA, 10.0s, Tokyo, 1964
- Charlie Greene, USA, 10.02s, Mexico City, 1968
- Armin Hary, Germany (FRG), 10.2s, Rome, 1960
- Ralphe Metcalfe, USA, 10.3s, Los Angeles, 1932
- Eddie Tolan, USA, 10.4s, Los Angeles, 1932
- Donald Lippincott, USA, 10.6s, Stockholm, 1912
- Frank Jarvis, USA, 10.8s, Paris, 1900

AMATEUR AND OLYMPIC SPORTS

QUESTIONS 478–480

478. Which games provided Canada with its best Winter Olympic medal count to date?
   A. Lillehammer
   B. Torino
   C. Sarajevo

479. In what sport has Canada won the most medals at the Winter Olympics?
   A. Ice hockey
   B. Figure skating
   C. Long track speed skating

480. Which Canadian speed skater holds the top three Olympic records in the women's 500 metres?
   A. Cindy Klassen
   B. Sylvie Daigle
   C. Catriona Le May Doan

Answers 478–480

478. B. Torino, Italy, 2006

Here is a list of Canada's most successful Olympic Winter Games:

- Torino, 2006, 24 medals (7 gold, 10 silver, 7 bronze)
- Salt Lake City, 2002, 17 medals (7 gold, 3 silver, 7 bronze)
- Nagano, 1998, 15 medals (6 gold, 5 silver, 4 bronze)
- Lillehammer, 1994, 13 medals (3 gold, 6 silver, 4 bronze)
- Albertville, 1992, 7 medals (2 gold, 3 silver, 2 bronze)
- Lake Placid, 1932, 7 medals (1 gold, 1 silver, 5 bronze)
- Calgary, 1988, 5 medals (0 gold, 2 silver, 3 bronze)
- Sarajevo, 1984, 4 medals (2 gold, 1 silver, 1 bronze)
- Squaw Valley, 1960, 4 medals (2 gold, 1 silver, 1 bronze)
- St. Moritz, 1948, 3 medals (2 gold, 0 silver, 1 bronze)

Note: Canada's total medal counts at Grenoble (1968), Innsbruck (1976), Cortina d'Ampezzo (1956) and Innsbruck (1964) are tied for the number 10 spot with St. Moritz. However, because at St. Moritz Canada won two gold medals and none of the others have more than one gold, St. Moritz sits alone at number 10 on my list.

479. C. Long track speed skating

Long track speed skating comes in first for Canada with 28 medals (6 gold, 10 silver, 12 bronze). Short track speed skating is second with 20 medals (5 gold, 8 silver, 7 bronze), and figure skating comes third with 20 medals (3 gold, 7 silver, 10 bronze).

480. C. Catriona Le May Doan

The long track speed skating record for this incredible athlete:

- 37.30s, Salt Lake City, 2002
- 38.21s, Nagano, 1998
- 38.39s, Nagano, 1998

American Bonnie Blair is a distant fourth, both in time (39.10s) and year (1988, Calgary).

QUESTIONS 481 – 482

481. Which Canadian male holds the Olympic record in short track speed skating's 500-metre event?
A. Marc Gagnon
B. Jonathan Guilmette
C. Jean-Francois Monette

482. Which Canadian athlete has won the most medals at the Olympics?
A. Marnie McBean
B. Marc Gagnon
C. Cindy Klassen

481. A. Marc Gagnon

The top 10 Olympic record holders in the men's short track 500-metre event are:

- Marc Gagnon, Canada, 41.802s, Salt Lake City, 2002
- Dong-Sung Kim, South Korea, 41.806s, Salt Lake City, 2002
- Jonathan Guilmette, Canada, 42.326s, Salt Lake City, 2002
- Takafumi Nishitani, Japan, 42.756s, Nagano, 1998
- Jiajun Li, China, 42.861s, Nagano, 1998
- Satoru Terao, Japan, 42.948s, Nagano, 1998
- Ji-Hoon Chae, South Korea, 43.45s, Lillehammer, 1994
- Mirko Vuillermin, Italy, 43.58s, Lillehammer, 1994
- Marc Gagnon, Canada, 43.84s, Lillehammer, 1994
- Bjornar Elgetun, Norway, 44.01s, Lillehammer, 1994

482. C. Cindy Klassen

Klassen was born in Winnipeg in 1979 and was an amazing speed skater. She has won 6 Olympic medals in all, 5 of which she won at the Torino Olympics in 2006. In 2002 she won her first Olympic medal, a bronze in the 3000 metres at Salt Lake City. Canada's top 10 medal-winning athletes are as follows:

- Cindy Klassen—long track speed skating, 6 medals (1 gold, 2 silver, 3 bronze)
- Marc Gagnon—short track speed skating, 5 medals (3 gold, 2 bronze)
- Clara Hughes—cycling, speed skating, 5 medals (1 gold, 1 silver, 3 bronze)
- Phillip Edwards—track and field, 5 bronze medals
- Kathleen Heddle—rowing, 4 medals (3 gold, 1 bronze)
- Marnie McBean—rowing, 4 medals (3 gold, 1 bronze)
- Eric Bedard—short track speed skating, 4 medals (2 gold, 1 silver, 1 bronze)
- Gaetan Boucher—long track speed skating, 4 medals (2 gold, 1 silver, 1 bronze)
- Victor Davis—swimming, 4 medals (1 gold, 3 silver)
- Lesley Thompson—rowing, 4 medals (1 gold, 2 silver, 1 bronze)

SCIENCE, INDUSTRY, INVENTION—AND THE GREATS INVOLVED IN EACH!

The firsts, the foremosts and the captains—all are the subject of this chapter's quiz. It's about those at the top of their game, the ones that were and are the most innovative, and especially those individuals who have ever dared to dream. We go from a little magazine and spectroscopy to baby food, space antennas and games of the tabletop, court or board varieties. It's a mixed bag to say the least, but at least it's a mixed bag of greats!

There is something to admire in all of these inventors, scientists, industrialists and their innovations and inventions. So study long and hard, and who knows, you might just be among these greats some day.

483. **The name of what Canadian science magazine refers to the time when the sun crosses the equator, and day and night are equal lengths?**
  A. *Tropic of Cancer*
  B. *Aurora*
  C. *Equinox*

484. **In 1944, what Ontario town became the site of the first nuclear reactor built outside the U.S.?**
  A. Chalk River
  B. Hamilton
  C. Pickering

ANSWERS 483 – 484

483. C. *Equinox*

484. A. Chalk River

SCIENCE, INDUSTRY, INVENTION—AND THE GREATS INVOLVED IN EACH!

Questions 485–488

485. What is the name of Ontario Power Generation's newest CANDU nuclear generating station?
- A. Pickering
- B. Bruce
- C. Darlington

486. In 1836, what future province became home to Canada's first railway?
- A. Ontario
- B. Québec
- C. New Brunswick

487. In 1846, Canada's first telegraph company began operation between what two Ontario locales?
- A. Toronto and Kingston
- B. Toronto and Ottawa
- C. Toronto and Hamilton

488. What German-born Canadian scientist won the 1971 Nobel Prize for Chemistry for his contributions to the field of atomic and molecular spectroscopy?
- A. James Franck
- B. Gerhard Herzberg
- C. Max Born

485. C. Darlington

486. B. Québec

The Champlain and Saint Lawrence Railroad, which began operation in 1836 (incorporated 1832), was Canada's first railway. It operated between La Prairie (just south of Montréal) and St. Jean on the Richelieu River.

487. C. Toronto and Hamilton

Established in late October 1846, The Toronto, Hamilton, Niagara and St. Catharines Telegraph company opened its first section between Toronto and Hamilton in December 1846.

488. B. Gerhard Herzberg

Born in Hamburg, Germany, in 1904, Herzberg was forced to leave Germany as a refugee in 1935. He worked as a guest professor at the University of Saskatchewan where he later became a professor of physics. In 1948, after a stint in Chicago, he returned to Canada and began working for the National Research Council.

SCIENCE, INDUSTRY, INVENTION—AND THE GREATS INVOLVED IN EACH!

QUESTIONS 489 – 492

489. In 1925, American-born Canadian manufacturer Gideon Sundback perfected what clothing fastener?
   A. Button
   B. Belt
   C. Zipper

490. What Canadian-born economic philosopher wrote *The Affluent Society*, which was originally published in 1958?
   A. John Kenneth Galbraith
   B. Gordon Pape
   C. Marshall McLuhan

491. In 1991, what despised tax was introduced in Canada with the rather false mantra "Revenue Neutral"?
   A. PST
   B. GST
   C. Countervailing Duty

492. Michael Budman and Don Green were the founders of what Canadian clothing chain that made a big splash for Canada's Olympic team in Nagano, Japan?
   A. Price Club
   B. The Body Shop
   C. Roots

Answers 489–492

489. C. Zipper
And yet the button-fly jean has become all the rage. Go figure!

490. A. John Kenneth Galbraith
His economic theories are classified as "liberal interventionist" and were displaced in the 1980s as conservative fundamentalism took hold…and failed.

491. B. GST
We can thank the neo-con government of Brian "I Love Money in Brown Envelopes" Mulroney for that one.

492. C. Roots
Roots has been making clothing for Olympians for some time, including jackets for the Jamaican bobsled team at the 1988 Winter Olympics in Calgary.

SCIENCE, INDUSTRY, INVENTION—AND THE GREATS INVOLVED IN EACH!

Questions 493–496

493. In 1997, what bridge opened that linked Prince Edward Island to New Brunswick by road for the first time?
 A. Confederation Bridge
 B. NBP Bridge
 C. Desjardins Canal Bridge

494. What Canadian business institution is the oldest incorporated joint-stock merchandising company in the English-speaking world?
 A. Canadian Tire
 B. Dominion
 C. Hudson's Bay Company

495. What Scottish-born Canadian inventor had an assistant named Thomas Watson?
 A. Alexander Graham Bell
 B. Gideon Sundback
 C. Joseph Armand Bombardier

496. Where was the world's first radio transmission received on December 12, 1901?
 A. St. John, New Brunswick
 B. St. John's, Newfoundland
 C. Halifax, Nova Scotia

Answers 493 – 496

493. A. Confederation Bridge

494. C. Hudson's Bay Company
The HBC was founded in 1670 when King Charles II of England granted a charter to his cousin Prince Rupert and his "Company of Adventurers." The charter granted HBC a monopoly on trade in Hudson Bay and ownership of all lands drained by rivers flowing into the bay.

495. A. Alexander Graham Bell

496. B. St. John's, Newfoundland
It was sent from Cornwall, England.

SCIENCE, INDUSTRY, INVENTION—AND THE GREATS INVOLVED IN EACH!

QUESTIONS 497 – 500

497. At Cabot Tower, which inventor received the first wireless telegraphic signals on December 12, 1901?
  A. Thomas Edison
  B. Guglielmo Marconi
  C. George Eastman

498. All nuclear power reactors in Canada are varying vintages of what type of reactor?
  A. Canadu reactors
  B. GoCan reactors
  C. CANDU reactors

499. The clock tower of what Canadian city's Old City Hall contains the third largest clock in the world after London's Big Ben (number two) and Shell-Mex Building (number one)?
  A. Montréal
  B. Ottawa
  C. Toronto

500. Alexander Graham Bell said the telephone was born in Boston, but was conceived in what Ontario city?
  A. Hamilton
  B. Brantford
  C. Burlington

497. B. Guglielmo Marconi

Marconi was an Italian inventor who shared the 1909 Nobel Prize in Physics with Karl Ferdinand Braun for their "contributions to the development of wireless telegraphy." A little-known fact is that Marconi later in life was quite active in the Italian Fascist movement.

498. C. CANDU reactors

CANDU stands for Canada Deuterium-Uranium and is a unique Canadian design. CANDU reactors use uranium as fuel and deuterium oxide (heavy water) as coolant.

499. C. Toronto

The clock in the bell tower at Toronto's Old City Hall was built by British clockmakers Gillette & Johnston. Toronto's clock has four faces with a dial that is 6 metres in diameter. Big Ben has a dial 7 metres in diameter, and the Shell-Mex building's clock has a face that is 7.6 metres in diameter. Toronto's clock first sounded at midnight on January 1, 1900.

500. B. Brantford

Brantford is the location of Bell's family home, and he spent much time there.

SCIENCE, INDUSTRY, INVENTION—AND THE GREATS INVOLVED IN EACH!

Questions 501 – 504

501. What dinosaur is named after a Canadian province?
   A. *Manitobatops*
   B. *Albertosaurus*
   C. *Kebec*

502. Alexander Graham Bell spent much of his life working as an advocate for people with what disability?
   A. Blindness
   B. Deafness
   C. Political aspirations

503. In 1967, with Quentin Fiore, who co-wrote the book *The Medium is the Message: An Inventory of Effects?*
   A. Marshall McLuhan
   B. John Kenneth Galbraith
   C. Don Cherry

504. Which Canadian organized the first mobile blood bank used on the battlefield?
   A. Wilder Penfield
   B. Norman Bethune
   C. Frederick Banting

WHAT IS CANADA?

Answers 501 – 504

501. B. *Albertosaurus*
It was a large meat-eater similar to the *Tyrannosaurus rex*.

502. B. Deafness
Bell's wife Mabel Garner Hubbard was deaf. He met her while he was working as a speech therapist for deaf people.

503. A. Marshall McLuhan
He became famous during the 1960s for studying mass media and its effects on thought and behaviour.

504. B. Norman Bethune

SCIENCE, INDUSTRY, INVENTION—AND THE GREATS INVOLVED IN EACH!

QUESTIONS 505–508

505. What indoor sport was invented by Canadian Thomas Ryan in 1909 and involves half as many objects for knocking down as in American and other versions of the game?

A. Five-pin bowling
B. Trivial Pursuit
C. Box lacrosse

506. What duo, along with their research team, isolated insulin in 1921?

A. Abbot and Costello
B. Diefenbaker and Pearson
C. Banting and Best

507. What Washington-based society known for its yellow border did Alexander Graham Bell become president of in 1898?

A. International Farmer's Union
B. AFL-CIO
C. National Geographic

508. In 1956 the first trans-Atlantic telephone cable was laid, running from Scotland to which Canadian province?

A. Nova Scotia
B. Québec
C. Newfoundland

505. A. Five-pin bowling

This version of bowling is apparently only played in Canada and came about as a result of laziness, of a sort. Apparently, customers at Thomas Ryan's Toronto Bowling Club complained that the 10-pin game was too strenuous. Ryan then cut down the pins, used smaller balls with lesser weights and bing, bang, boom, the Canadian variant was created, basically.

506. C. Banting and Best

Dr. Frederick Banting and Dr. Charles Best isolated insulin while working together at the University of Toronto. The drug, as we all know, revolutionized the treatment of diabetes.

507. C. National Geographic

508. C. Newfoundland

Prior to 1956, trans-Atlantic telephone service was radio based. The idea of running cable under water had been discussed earlier, but some technological innovations were needed. The first trans-Atlantic cable was laid between Gallanch Bay near Oban, Scotland, and Clarenville, Newfoundland. It was known as TAT-1. Use of the cable was discontinued in 1978.

SCIENCE, INDUSTRY, INVENTION—AND THE GREATS INVOLVED IN EACH!

QUESTIONS 509–512

509. What Scottish-born Canadian inventor and civil engineer played a key role in developing a worldwide system of standard time as well as designing Canada's first postage stamp?
   A. Ian Fleming
   B. Sir Sandford Fleming
   C. Sir Alexander Fleming

510. Who invented the snowmobile, in 1937?
   A. Joseph Armand Bombardier
   B. James Abbot
   C. Alexander Graham Bell

511. In 1939, Dr. W.R. Franks invented what type of suit that allowed pilots to withstand higher centrifugal forces without passing out?
   A. Diving suit
   B. Anti-gravity suit
   C. Double-breasted suit

512. What type of snow shovel was invented in 1869 by J.W. Elliot of Toronto?
   A. Revolving snow shovel
   B. Handled snow shovel
   C. Plastic snow shovel

Answers 509–512

509. B. Sir Sandford Fleming

Canada's first postage stamp was the three-penny beaver, which was issued in 1851.

510. A. Joseph Armand Bombardier

Bombardier's innovation was in using skis to steer the vehicle in front of a tracked drive. By 1947 he had created a 12-passenger vehicle that had mainly military uses. By 1959 Bombardier also offered a personal snowmobile called a Ski-Doo, which took off partly as a new winter sport and partly as new markets opened among Inuit people in the North.

511. B. Anti-gravity suit

Dr. Franks and his colleagues developed the anti-gravity suit at the University of Toronto. It is the forerunner to spacesuits worn by astronauts today.

512. A. Revolving snow shovel

It was the forerunner of the rotary snow plow, which is used all over the world today.

SCIENCE, INDUSTRY, INVENTION—AND THE GREATS INVOLVED IN EACH!

QUESTIONS 513–516

513. What software developer invented the Java programming language in 1991?
   A. Bill Gates
   B. James Gosling
   C. Steve Jobs

514. What American-born Canadian physician discovered that electrical stimulation of the brain aided in the treatment of epilepsy?
   A. John Polanyi
   B. William Osler
   C. Wilder Penfield

515. What prolific Canadian design engineer was born in Hamilton, Ontario, and worked on many inventions ranging from a wheelchair for quadriplegics to the National Research Council's first wind tunnels, and consulted on the gear design for the Canadarm?
   A. George Klein
   B. John Polanyi
   C. William Osler

516. What baby food was invented by Dr. Alan Brown, Dr. Fred Tisdall and Dr. Theo Drake?
   A. Gerbers
   B. Oatmeal
   C. Pablum

Answers 513–516

513. B. James Gosling
He was born near Calgary in 1955. With Sun Microsystems since 1984, Gosling invented Java in 1991.

514. C. Wilder Penfield
A visual demonstration of his work can be seen in a Canadian History vignette where Dr. Penfield is dramatized as he stimulates a female patient's brain during surgery, and she says: "Dr. Penfield, I can smell burnt toast."

515. A. George Klein
During World War II, Klein designed aiming systems for artillery as well as naval mortars. He invented a radio antenna that could be retracted onto a reel (called a STEM) that was first used on the Alouette satellite in 1962. He was also on the team that designed the first atomic reactor outside the United States.

516. C. Pablum
The three pediatricians, with help from others, created the cereal Pablum, which was revolutionary because it helped prevent rickets by ensuring children had sufficient amounts of vitamin D. For 25 years the Hospital for Sick Children (Toronto) received a royalty on every package of Pablum that was sold. The brand was acquired by the H.J. Heinz Company in 2005.

SCIENCE, INDUSTRY, INVENTION—AND THE GREATS INVOLVED IN EACH!

QUESTIONS 517 – 520

517. Donald Munro is thought to have invented what tabletop version of one of Canada's national sports?
   A. Lacrosse
   B. Hockey
   C. Bowling

518. Donald Hings developed one of the earliest of portable communication devices that are commonly called what?
   A. Cell phones
   B. Communicators
   C. Walkie talkies

519. Chris Haney and Scott Abbott invented what very popular board game in 1979?
   A. Trivial Pursuit
   B. Boggle
   C. Yahtzee

520. Who invented the McIntosh variety of apples?
   A. Richard McIntosh
   B. John Richards
   C. John McIntosh

ANSWERS 517–520

517. B. Hockey
You all know this tabletop game. It's hockey played on a miniature replica ice rink with players mounted an small spikes that can be moved or spun around by steel rods. Donald Munro of Toronto apparently invented this version of the game way back in 1932.

518. C. Walkie talkies
The first of these devices that Hings developed was a portable, emergency voice radio for pilots working in the mining industry. The device could float and had a folding antenna, and its signal could reach up to 200 kilometres. The British military became interested in Hings' invention. The actual name came about when a soldier who was asked to describe what it does apparently replied something about being able to walk while one talks into it.

519. A. Trivial Pursuit
Scott Abbott was a sports editor with the *Canadian Press*, and Chris Haney was a photo editor for the *Montréal Gazette*.

520. C. John McIntosh
Although he was born in the Mohawk Valley of New York state, John McIntosh moved to Canada West in 1796. By 1811, he moved to Dundela, Iroquois, in Canada West, where he and his son Allan eventually grafted and cultivated the McIntosh red apple, which was originally known as Granny. The original McIntosh apple tree produced fruit for more than 90 years. It died in 1910, 65 years after John McIntosh himself died.

SCIENCE, INDUSTRY, INVENTION—AND THE GREATS
INVOLVED IN EACH!

QUESTIONS 521–523

521. Canada's Graeme Ferguson co-invented what movie system?
  A. Digital film
  B. IMAX
  C. 16 mm

522. Which soft drink was created by pharmacist John J. McLaughlin in 1904?
  A. Coca Cola
  B. Pepsi-Cola
  C. Canada Dry Pale Ginger Ale

523. Who invented the sport of basketball?
  A. Alan Smithee
  B. Tab Hunter
  C. James Naismith

521. B. IMAX

IMAX stands for Image Maximization. It was developed by Ferguson, Roman Kroiter, Robert Kerr and engineer William Shaw. IMAX is double the size of traditional 35 mm film and because of that needed both a new camera and projection system developed. It premiered at the Osaka World's Fair in 1970. The first IMAX film was made by legendary Canadian filmmaker Donald Brittain and it is titled *Tiger Child* (1970).

522. C. Canada Dry Pale Ginger Ale

John J. McLaughlin was the son of Robert McLaughlin who, as owner of McLaughlin Motor Car, had the largest such business in the British Empire. In 1890 John opened a carbonated water plant in Toronto. He created his famed Ginger Ale in 1904, but it was when he began shipping it to New York in 1919 that it really took off. It was so successful that John opened a plant in Manhattan. The company and the product are now part of Cadbury-Schweppes.

523. C. James Naismith

(I thought I'd throw you a couple of easy questions to round out this chapter. At least I hope they were easy.)

ART, LITERATURE AND ENTERTAINMENT

This chapter is a grab bag of all things entertaining, but nothing in the realm of Canadians eating their young. All these really nifty and neato questions and answers will have an artistic and entertaining bent. From movies to TV to literature, writin' of a less lofty sort and other forms of broadcasting, as well as yer high falutin' films, meaningful stories and the people who create them, produce them and spin them the best they can. We've also got some belters, and by that I do mean singers. There are definitely some powerful lungs in this country, and I'm sure if I didn't touch on a few of them I would hear about it...in a REALLY LOUD way!

What I've tried to do, and what I think you might notice, is I've kept it to entertainment-related people, stories, songs and the like that have some legs or staying power. The flash-in-the-pans and the ones who haven't been around long enough, I've shied away from. You won't find the obscure ones, just those that most of us with a general sense of things know in a most common and entertaining sort of way. With that in mind, you'll probably be amazed at how much Canadian entertaining, entertainers, and even artists there are. I know I was.

So, stop stalling. Go forth and answer some questions. It's a big country and a big chapter. Get to it!

524. In 1961, what Canadian author self-published her first collection of poems called *Double Persephone*?

A. Alice Munro
B. Margaret Atwood
C. Margaret Laurence

524. B. Margaret Atwood

ART, LITERATURE AND ENTERTAINMENT

QUESTIONS 525–528

525. Which Hollywood actor mainly known for comedies has a brother named Erik who was a federal Cabinet minister in the Brian Mulroney government?
    A. Jim Carrey
    B. Michael J. Fox
    C. Leslie Nielsen

526. Who played the title characters in "Thirty Two Short Films about Glenn Gould" (1993) and in "Trudeau," a 2002 mini-series?
    A. Colm Feore
    B. Colm Meaney
    C. Colm Wilkinson

527. In August 2006, what Canadian supermodel came out of retirement at age 41 to grace the cover of *Vogue* magazine?
    A. Yasmeen Ghauri
    B. Linda Evangelista
    C. Shalom Harlow

528. Who is the lead singer of Canada's The Tragically Hip?
    A. Chad Kroeger
    B. Ronnie Hawkins
    C. Gord Downie

525. C. Leslie Nielsen

His brother is former Deputy Prime Minister Erik Nielson.

526. A. Colm Feore

Feore has had a stellar career in film, TV and on the stage. He was actually born in Boston, Massachusetts, though his family settled in Ottawa when he was three years old.

527. B. Linda Evangelista

She was pregnant at the time of the photo shoot and gave birth to her son, Austin James, on October 11 of the same year.

528. C. Gord Downie

ART, LITERATURE AND ENTERTAINMENT

Questions 529 – 532

529. In what city would you find Sonja Bata's shoe museum?
   A. Ottawa
   B. Vancouver
   C. Toronto

530. What Canadian-born actress was ape-gripped by an oversized gorilla in the 1933 film *King Kong*?
   A. Fay Wray
   B. Margot Kidder
   C. Jessica Lange

531. What current "back to the land" magazine is named after the Ontario town from which it originates?
   A. *Toronto Life*
   B. *Vancouver Today*
   C. *Harrowsmith*

532. In 2001, what Canadian author wrote, *Marching As To War*?
   A. Farley Mowat
   B. Pierre Berton
   C. Arthur Black

Answers 529–532

529. C. Toronto
The Bata Shoe Museum building was designed by Canadian architect Raymond Moriyama and is meant to kind of look like a shoe box that is being opened.

530. A. Fay Wray
Wray proved she had quite the set of pipes on her with all the screaming she did in the film. She was born in Cardston, Alberta, in 1907. She died in 2004. The lights of the Empire State Building in New York City were dimmed for 15 minutes in August 2004 to honour her. She has a star on Hollywood's Walk of Fame and another on Canada's Walk of Fame in Toronto, which was awarded posthumously in 2005.

531. C. *Harrowsmith*
The magazine's full name is *Harrowsmith Country Life*.

532. B. Pierre Berton
It describes how war helped Canada become an independent nation, breaking free of Great Britain and forging a love-hate relationship with the United States.

ART, LITERATURE AND ENTERTAINMENT

QUESTIONS 533–536

533. What Canadian-born actor starred as the title character in the 1997 James Bond parody film *Austin Powers: International Man of Mystery?*
  A. Mike Myers
  B. Ryan Gosling
  C. Jim Carrey

534. What old Toronto concert auditorium is named after a Canadian family associated with farm machinery?
  A. Roy Thomson Hall
  B. Rogers Centre
  C. Massey Hall

535. What sport was the subject of the 2002 film *Men with Brooms,* which starred and was directed by Paul Gross?
  A. Curling
  B. Football
  C. Basketball

536. Who wrote *Anne of Green Gables,* which was originally published in 1908?
  A. Mark Twain
  B. Margaret Atwood
  C. Lucy Maud Montgomery

WHAT IS CANADA?

ANSWERS 533 – 536

533. A. Mike Myers
He also wrote the screenplay and played Dr. Evil in the film.

534. C. Massey Hall

535. A. Curling

536. C. Lucy Maud Montgomery
Of course, *Anne of Green Gables* has gone on to spawn (and I do mean spawn) a whole industry surrounding it, including plays, movies and TV series.

ART, LITERATURE AND ENTERTAINMENT

Questions 537–540

537. Who wrote a 1986 novel about Noah and his family entitled *Not Wanted on the Voyage*?
   A. Mordecai Richler
   B. Paul Quarrington
   C. Timothy Findley

538. Tom Thomson was a forerunner of what association of artists founded in 1920?
   A. Impressionists
   B. Group of Seven
   C. Fauvists

539. In his 2002 memoir *Lucky Man*, what Canadian-born actor and star of the *Back to the Future* films chronicled his fight with Parkinson's disease?
   A. Michael J. Fox
   B. Russel Peters
   C. Jim Carrey

540. In 1999, who recorded the pop songs "When You're Gone" and "Cloud #9"?
   A. Lee Aaron
   B. Burton Cummings
   C. Bryan Adams

WHAT IS CANADA?

Answers 537 – 540

537. C. Timothy Findley
He died in 2002.

538. B. Group of Seven

539. A. Michael J. Fox
The book's full title is *Lucky Man: A Memoir*.

540. C. Bryan Adams

ART, LITERATURE AND ENTERTAINMENT

QUESTIONS 541–544

541. Which Canadian author was born in Pittsburgh, Pennsylvania, studied to become a Jesuit priest and wrote the children's stories "Dave's Father," "Mud Puddle" and "Love You Forever"?
   A. Mike Ulmer
   B. Robert Munsch
   C. Mordecai Richler

542. What Canadian filmmaker directed Cher to an Oscar win in the 1987 film *Moonstruck*?
   A. Norman Jewison
   B. Sarah Polley
   C. David Cronenberg

543. Which Canadian author of the 1908-published novel *Sowing Seeds in Danny* was instrumental in winning women the right to vote in both Alberta and Manitoba?
   A. Nellie McClung
   B. Emily Murphy
   C. Louise McKinney

544. What Inuit film won the 2001 Camera D'or for Best Feature Film at the Cannes international film festival?
   A. *Atanarjuat*
   B. *Cool Runnings*
   C. *The Fast Runner*

541. B. Robert Munsch

Munsch traces his storytelling back to 1972 when he left the Jesuits to work full time in a daycare. It wasn't until he was working in a daycare lab at the University of Guelph that he published his first story, "Mud Puddle." He is probably best known for his book, *Love You Forever*, which topped the *New York Times* bestseller list in 1994 and has never been out of print.

542. A. Norman Jewison

The film also starred Nicholas Cage, Danny Aiello and Olympia Dukakis.

543. A. Nellie McClung

McClung was one of the "Famous Five"—five visionary women from Alberta who fought to have women recognized as persons by the British North America Act. The Famous Five were Nellie McClung, Emily Murphy, Louise McKinney, Henrietta Muir Edwards and Irene Parlby.

544. A. *Atanarjuat* or C. *The Fast Runner*

Both answers are correct, since the English title of the Inuit film *Atanarjuat* is *The Fast Runner*.

ART, LITERATURE AND ENTERTAINMENT

QUESTIONS 545 – 549

545. Who was the youngest member of the Group of Seven painters and the last of the group to die?
   A. Franklin Carmichael
   B. A.J. Casson
   C. Frederick Varley

546. Who played the title character in the 2003 film *The Cat in the Hat?*
   A. Mike Myers
   B. Jim Carrey
   C. Dan Aykroyd

547. Who won the 2002 Man Booker Prize for the novel *Life of Pi?*
   A. Michael Ondaatje
   B. Yann Martel
   C. Irving Layton

548. Who directed the 1997 film *The Sweet Hereafter?*
   A. Atom Egoyan
   B. David Cronenberg
   C. Anne Wheeler

549. What 1995 Michael Moore–directed film was sort of comedic and starred John Candy?
   A. *Canadian Bacon*
   B. *Porky's*
   C. *Sicko*

ANSWERS 545 – 549

545. B. A.J. Casson

Casson died in February 1992. He was not one of the original members of the Group of Seven. Frank Johnston (one of the original Group of Seven) left the group in 1921, and in 1926, Casson was asked to join. The original members of the Group of Seven were Franklin Carmichael, Lawren Harris, A.Y. Jackson, Frank Johnston, Arthur Lismer, J.E.H. MacDonald and Frederick Varley. Edwin Holgate was asked to join the group in 1930; Lionel LeMoine Fitzgerald was asked to join the group in 1932 after J.E.H. MacDonald died.

546. A. Mike Myers

547. B. Yann Martel

Martel was born in Salamanca, Spain, in 1963. *Life of Pi* involves a boy being shipwrecked and set adrift in a lifeboat with a Bengal tiger as well as other animals.

548. A. Atom Egoyan

The film is not so much sweet, but on the bright side, it does seem to go on forever, leading to the hereafter.

549. A. *Canadian Bacon*

ART, LITERATURE AND ENTERTAINMENT

QUESTIONS 550–553

550. What 1998 film spans five countries over three centuries and has a violin as the main character?
- A. *The Tin Drum*
- B. *The Red Violin*
- C. *Tomb Raider*

551. What Nova Scotia–born author wrote the 1941 novel *Barometer Rising,* which focuses on the Halifax explosion in 1917?
- A. Hugh MacLennan
- B. Hugh Garner
- C. Gabrielle Roy

552. Which novel by Timothy Findley uses Ezra Pound's fictional character, Hugh Selwyn Mauberly, as its main character?
- A. *Famous Last Words*
- B. *Headhunter*
- C. *The Wars*

553. In what city is the National Gallery of Canada?
- A. Ottawa
- B. Toronto
- C. Montréal

WHAT IS CANADA?

ANSWERS 550–553

550. B. *The Red Violin*

551. A. Hugh MacLennan

552. A. *Famous Last Words*
The character, Hugh Selwyn Mauberly, is taken from Ezra Pound's poem, which also has the title "Famous Last Words."

553. A. Ottawa

ART, LITERATURE AND ENTERTAINMENT

QUESTIONS 554–557

554. In 1873, who wrote about Sir Sandford Fleming's overland journey to the Pacific in the book *Ocean to Ocean*?
   A. Katherine Parr Trail
   B. Reverend George Monro Grant
   C. Susanna Moodie

555. What Hollywood actor grew up in Toronto, played Neo in three *Matrix* movies and starred as Hamlet for the Manitoba Theatre Centre in 1995?
   A. Keanu Reeves
   B. Eugene Levy
   C. Andrea Martin

556. Who wrote the 1945-published novel *Bonheur d'occasion,* which was translated into English as *The Tin Flute*?
   A. Roch Carrier
   B. Gabrielle Roy
   C. Patrick Roy

557. Who wrote the "The Wreck of the Edmund Fitzgerald" and released it as a song in 1976?
   A. Anne Murray
   B. Great Big Sea
   C. Gordon Lightfoot

554. B. Reverend George Monro Grant

Grant was born in Nova Scotia in 1835. He accompanied Sir Sandford Fleming on his trip across Canada and wrote about it in *Ocean to Ocean*. Reverend Grant was a principal of Queen's University in Kingston.

555. A. Keanu Reeves

556. B. Gabrielle Roy

557. C. Gordon Lightfoot

ART, LITERATURE AND ENTERTAINMENT

Questions 558 – 560

558. What is the name of the theatre located seven stories above Toronto's Elgin Theatre?
A. Winter Garden
B. Pantagess
C. Princess of Wales

559. What cheekily named music group was once banned from performing at Toronto's New Years Eve celebration at Nathan Philips Square?
A. Nickelback
B. Barenaked Ladies
C. Cowboy Junkies

560. The film version of which Michael Ondaatje novel earned nine Oscars at the 1997 Academy Awards?
A. *In the Skin of a Lion*
B. *Anil's Ghost*
C. *The English Patient*

WHAT IS CANADA?

ANSWERS 558 – 560

558. A. Winter Garden

Toronto's Elgin and Winter Garden theatres are the last surviving Edwardian stacked theatres in the world. They were originally built in 1913. The lower Elgin Theatre is ornate and was originally called Loew's Yonge Street Theatre. Vaudeville productions as well as plays were produced in the Elgin, and some of the world's top talent performed there. The upper theatre, the Winter Garden, is decorated in such a way that it resembles a forest. It was built to house mainly vaudeville productions.

559. B. Barenaked Ladies

In 1991 a staffer at city hall saw the BNL name listed as performing at the New Years Eve bash, but had them removed from the bill because it was thought their name objectified women. Of course, the band's name was meant in fun as many of their songs attest. The media circus that erupted around the controversy helped get BNL recognition and success was just around the corner. The group was originally made up of Jim Creeggan, Steven Page, Ed Robertson, Tyler Stewart and Jim's brother, Andy Creeggan. Andy Creeggan left the group and was replaced by Kevin Hearn.

560. C. *The English Patient*

The film was released in 1996 and directed by Anthony Minghella. It starred Ralph Fiennes, Kristin Scott Thomas, Juliette Binoche and Colin Firth. At the Academy Awards, the film was nominated for 12 Oscars and won nine.

ART, LITERATURE AND ENTERTAINMENT

Questions 561–564

561. What Toronto-born American architect designed a recent addition for the Art Gallery of Ontario, as well as the Disney Concert Theatre in Los Angeles and the Guggenheim Museum in Bilbao, Spain?
   A. Arthur Erickson
   B. Frank Gehry
   C. Douglas Cardinal

562. What Ottawa-born entertainer was one of many stars of the 1962 film *The Longest Day*, and wrote and released the hit song "Diana" in 1957?
   A. Neil Sedaka
   B. Burton Cummings
   C. Paul Anka

563. Who wrote the novel *The Loved and the Lost*, published in 1951?
   A. Morley Callaghan
   B. Barry Callaghan
   C. Rick Mercer

564. What long-running quiz show was created by Merv Griffin and has been hosted by Canadian-born Alex Trebek since 1984?
   A. *Wheel of Fortune*
   B. *Jeopardy*
   C. *TimeChase*

WHAT IS CANADA?

ANSWERS 561 – 564

561. B. Frank Gehry

Gehry is a past winner of the Pritzker Prize, arguably the most prestigious honour any architect can win. Interestingly Frank Gehry won the Pritzker in 1989, before some of his most famous projects were conceived or built. Gehry's addition to the Art Gallery of Ontario is scheduled to be completed in the fall of 2008.

562. C. Paul Anka

563. A. Morley Callaghan

564. B. *Jeopardy*

ART, LITERATURE AND ENTERTAINMENT

QUESTIONS 565 – 568

565. What Toronto-born writer, producer and performer starred as the inept handyman named Red Green on TV and in the 2002 film *Duct Tape Forever?*
  A. Gordon Pinsent
  B. Paul Gross
  C. Steve Smith

566. Who was named a Companion of the Order of Canada in 1968 and also portrayed Captain Von Trapp in the 1965 film *The Sound of Music?*
  A. Al Waxman
  B. Lorne Greene
  C. Christopher Plummer

567. What is illuminated by the sun each November 11 at 11:00 AM at Canada's War Museum in Ottawa?
  A. Sherman Tank
  B. Ross Rifle
  C. Headstone of Canada's Unknown Soldier

568. What sketch comedy show originally aired on TV in different incarnations from 1976 to 1984 and starred John Candy, Joe Flaherty, Eugene Levy, Andrea Martin, Rick Moranis, Catherine O'Hara, Harold Ramis, Martin Short and Dave Thomas as well as Robin Duke and Tony Rosato?
  A. *Saturday Night Live*
  B. *SCTV*
  C. *Night Heat*

WHAT IS CANADA?

Answers 565 – 568

565. C. Steve Smith

A comedic genius!

566. C. Christopher Plummer

He was born in Toronto in 1929 and has had a long, successful and eclectic career playing fictional characters such as Sherlock Holmes (*Murder by Decree*) and a Klingon in *Star Trek VI: The Undiscovered Country*, as well as portraying real people, such as Mike Wallace (*The Insider*) and Prime Minister Sir John A. Macdonald (*Riel*).

567. C. Headstone of Canada's Unknown Soldier

The museum was designed by Raymond Moriyama with the theme of regeneration.

568. B. SCTV

The show is set at the fictional SCTV television station in Melonville. There was an ongoing soap opera called "The Days of the Week" and recurring characters such as sleazy Johnny LaRue (Candy), owner Guy Caballero (Flaherty), station manager Edith Prickley (Martin), Bob & Doug MacKenzie (Moranis and Thomas), performer Lola Heatherton (O'Hara), news anchors Floyd Robertson and Earl Camembert (Flaherty and Levy), and various Martin Short characters, including Ed Grimley. The actors also did some dead-on impersonations of Bob Hope (Thomas), Ricardo Mantalban (Levy), Katharine Hepburn (O'Hara), Woody Allen (Moranis), Mother Theresa (Andrea Martin), and William F. Buckley Jr. (Flaherty). SCTV was one of the earliest examples of a Canadian show that was actually popular with Canadian viewers. I also loved this show and still do!

ART, LITERATURE AND ENTERTAINMENT

QUESTIONS 569–572

569. Based on a novel by E. Anne Proulx, what 2001 film starred Kevin Spacey and Julianne Moore and was set in Newfoundland?
   A. *The Shipping News*
   B. *Dolores Claiborne*
   C. *Brokeback Mountain*

570. Who wrote the children's book *Jacob Two-Two Meets the Hooded Fang*, as well as the adult novel *Joshua Then and Now*?
   A. Clark Blaise
   B. Will Ferguson
   C. Mordecai Richler

571. Which author wrote *Nonsense Novels* in 1911, *Arcadian Adventures with the Idle Rich* in 1914, and has the Canadian medal for Humour Writing in Book Form named for him?
   A. Stephen Leacock
   B. Harry Symons
   C. Paul Hiebert

572. What Alberta-born architect designed the Canadian Museum of Civilization located in Hull, Québec?
   A. Arthur Erickson
   B. Douglas Cardinal
   C. Frank Gehry

WHAT IS CANADA?

Answers 569–572

569. A. *The Shipping News*

570. C. Mordecai Richler

Richler was born and raised in Montréal. He lived in Paris in the early 1950s. In 1954 his first novel, *The Acrobats,* was published. He published many novels and essays over the years and had a particular love-hate relationship with Québec, but especially separatists. He died in 2001. His last novels were *Solomon Gursky Was Here* (1989), for which he won the Commonwealth Writers Prize in 1990, and *Barney's Version* (1997).

571. A. Stephen Leacock

Leacock was a prolific writer on many subjects, including economics and political science. He was probably best known in his time for his essays, stories and books of humour. Each spring the Stephen Leacock Foundation awards one book from the previous year for the Stephen Leacock Memorial Medal for Humour. Of the multiple-choice answers I gave you for this question, Harry Symons was the very first winner of the Leacock Medal. He won the award in 1947 for *Ojibway Melody*. The second winner of the award was Paul Hiebert in 1948 for his book *Sarah Binks*. A great many fine Canadian writers have won the Leacock Medal, including Earle Birney, Robertson Davies, Pierre Berton, W.O. Mitchell, Farley Mowat, Gary Lautens, W.P. Kinsella, Arthur Black and Stuart McLean.

572. B. Douglas Cardinal

ART, LITERATURE AND ENTERTAINMENT

QUESTIONS 573–576

573. What Saskatchewan-born author wrote *Who Has Seen the Wind* and *Jake and the Kid*?
  A. W.P. Kinsella
  B. Will Ferguson
  C. W.O. Mitchell

574. What Manitoba-born author wrote *The Stone Angel* in 1964 and *The Diviners* in 1974?
  A. Margaret Laurence
  B. Margaret Atwood
  C. Alice Munro

575. What often-parodied Canadian singer was born the youngest of 14 children in Charlemagne, Québec, in 1968, has performed for the Pope and sang the ballad "My Heart Will Go On" for the 1997 film *Titanic*?
  A. Anne Murray
  B. Rita MacNeil
  C. Celine Dion

576. Which Hollywood mogul was born in Russia, grew up in St. John, New Brunswick, and ran MGM for many years?
  A. Louis B. Mayer
  B. Irving Thalberg
  C. Jack Warner

ANSWERS 573 – 576

573. C. W.O. Mitchell
After a prolific writing career, Mitchell died in Calgary in 1998.

574. A. Margaret Laurence

575. C. Celine Dion
In 1994, she married her long-time manager (from the age she was 12), Rene Angelil.

576. A. Louis B. Mayer

ART, LITERATURE AND ENTERTAINMENT

QUESTIONS 577–580

577. What Canadian broadcaster has won the Stephen Leacock Medal for Humour and written the books *Arthur! Arthur!* and *Flashblack?*
   A. Stuart McLean
   B. Will Ferguson
   C. Arthur Black

578. What Canadian producer created the NBC late-night TV show *Saturday Night Live?*
   A. Dick Ebersol
   B. Andrew Alexander
   C. Lorne Michaels

579. What Canadian-born actress appeared with Greta Garbo in *Anna Christie* and won an Academy Award in 1931 for *Min and Bill?*
   A. Marie Dressler
   B. Norma Shearer
   C. Fay Wray

580. What Canadian singer was born in Springhill, Nova Scotia, in 1945 and has had hits with songs such as "Snowbird," "You Needed Me" and "I Just Fall in Love Again"?
   A. Rita MacNeil
   B. Anne Murray
   C. Avril Lavigne

Answers 577–580

577. C. Arthur Black
He hosted the CBC radio show Basic Black for many years and has won the Stephen Leacock Medal for Humour three times.

578. C. Lorne Michaels

579. A. Marie Dressler
She was born in Cobourg, Ontario, in 1868 and won the Academy Award for Best Actress in 1931, playing opposite Wallace Beery in *Min and Bill*.

580. B. Anne Murray

ART, LITERATURE AND ENTERTAINMENT

QUESTIONS 581–584

581. What Canadian sketch comedy TV series grew out of a comedy troupe from Newfoundland of the same name and starred Tommy Sexton, Greg Malone, Cathy Jones, Mary Walsh and Andy Jones?
   A. *CODCO*
   B. *Monday Report*
   C. *This Hour Has 22 Minutes*

582. Who won the Governor General's Literary Award for *Dance of the Happy Shades*, which was published in 1968?
   A. Alice Munro
   B. Margaret Atwood
   C. Margaret Laurence

583. What CBC-radio broadcaster won the Stephen Leacock Award for Humour three times and wrote the books *Secrets from the Vinyl Café* and *Vinyl Café Diaries*?
   A. Peter Gzowski
   B. Ian Ferguson
   C. Stuart McLean

584. What Canadian rock band included Burton Cummings and Randy Bachman as members and had hits with "American Woman" and "No Sugar Tonight"?
   A. BTO
   B. Goddo
   C. The Guess Who

ANSWERS 581 – 584

581. A. CODCO
Robert Joy was also in the original *CODCO* troupe, but he was not part of the TV show.

582. A. Alice Munro

583. C. Stuart McLean
He is tied with fellow CBC broadcaster Arthur Black in winning the Stephen Leacock Award the most times. Each has been a "three-peat."

584. C. The Guess Who

ART, LITERATURE AND ENTERTAINMENT

QUESTIONS 585 – 588

585. What Canadian country-rock band counts Jim Cuddy and Greg Keelor as members?
   A. Blue Rodeo
   B. Nickelback
   C. The Stampeders

586. Once known as America's Sweetheart, what Academy Award–winning actress was born in Toronto as Gladys Louise Smith?
   A. Norma Shearer
   B. Mary Pickford
   C. Lilliane Gish

587. What Canadian comedy troupe—and stars of radio and television—count Don Ferguson and Luba Goy as members?
   A. Kids in the Hall
   B. Dead Cooks
   C. Royal Canadian Air Farce

588. What 1960s singing group included members John Phillips, Cass Elliot, Michelle Phillips as well as Canadian Denny Doherty?
   A. The Mamas & The Papas
   B. The Lovin' Spoonful
   C. The Beatles

Answers 585 – 588

585. A. Blue Rodeo

586. B. Mary Pickford

She won the Academy Award for Best Actress in 1929 for *Coquette*. She was also a founder of United Artists with her husband Douglas Fairbanks, along with Charlie Chaplin and D.W. Griffiths.

587. C. Royal Canadian Air Farce

Original members included Roger Abbott, Don Ferguson, Luba Goy, John Morgan and Dave Broadfoot as well as writers Gord Holtam and Rick Olsen.

588. A. The Mamas & The Papas

ART, LITERATURE AND ENTERTAINMENT

QUESTIONS 589–592

589. What British Columbia–born composer and musician wrote the theme song for the 1988 Winter Olympics in Calgary?
   A. David Foster
   B. Alan Thicke
   C. Bryan Adams

590. What 1977 Canadian film about a drag queen and his schizophrenic friend starred Hollis McLaren and Craig Russell and was a surprising hit?
   A. *Goin' Down the Road*
   B. *Riel*
   C. *Outrageous!*

591. What Vancouver-born architect designed or co-designed BC's Simon Fraser University, the Canadian Embassy in Washington, DC, and Roy Thompson Hall in Toronto?
   A. Arthur Erickson
   B. Geoffrey Massey
   C. Moshe Safdie

592. What American quiz show phenomenon had a short-lived Canadian spinoff in the year 2000 that was hosted by journalist Pamela Wallin?
   A. *Jeopardy*
   B. *Who Wants To Be a Millionaire*
   C. *Deal or No Deal*

Answers 589–592

589. A. David Foster

590. C. *Outrageous!*
The film was directed by Kentucky-born writer-director Dick Benner and was based on a short story by the late Margaret Gibson.

591. A. Arthur Erickson

592. B. *Who Wants To Be a Millionaire*
At that time, the Canadian Version of *Who Wants To Be a Millionaire* received the highest ratings ever for a network production…and CTV was so savvy about it they failed to follow up or do anything else about bringing the show back.

ART, LITERATURE AND ENTERTAINMENT

QUESTIONS 593–596

593. What female country singer was born in Edmonton, grew up in Consort, Alberta, and recorded the rock-and-roll ballad "Crying" as a duet with Roy Orbison in 1987?
  A. Sarah McLachlan
  B. k.d. lang
  C. Shania Twain

594. What widely produced Canadian play about a fighter pilot was co-written by John MacLachlan Gray and Eric Peterson and premiered in Vancouver in 1978?
  A. "The Drowsy Chaperone"
  B. "Billy Bishop Goes to War"
  C. "2 Pianos 4 Hands"

595. What Canadian filmmaker wrote and directed the 1986 film *Le declin de l'empire américain* (*The Decline of the American Empire*)?
  A. Brad Fraser
  B. Jean-Claude Lauzon
  C. Denys Arcand

596. Which Canadian actress was born in Yellowknife, appeared in the 1974 horror flick *Black Christmas* and starred opposite Christopher Reeve in four *Superman* movies?
  A. Margot Kidder
  B. Helen Shaver
  C. Carrie-Anne Moss

Answers 593–596

593. B. k.d. lang
The "k.d." stands for her name, Kathryn Dawn, not Kraft Dinner.

594. B. "Billy Bishop Goes to War"
The other two choices in the question are also quite successful Canadian musicals. The play "2 Pianos 4 Hands" was created and performed by Richard Greenblatt and Ted Dykstra. The "Drowsy Chaperone" might be the most successful Canadian play or musical to ever go to Broadway. The book for Drowsy was written by Bob Martin and Don McKellar, and the music and lyrics were written by Lisa Lambert and Greg Morrison. Drowsy originated in Toronto as a Fringe Festival production and went on to win five Tony Awards on Broadway. It was actually nominated for 13 Tonys.

595. C. Denys Arcand
The Decline of the American Empire won the Critics Prize at the Cannes Film Festival (1986) and numerous other prizes for Arcand.

596. A. Margot Kidder

ART, LITERATURE AND ENTERTAINMENT

QUESTIONS 597–599

597. What architect was born in Haifa, Israel, in 1938, grew up in Montréal and designed both Habitat '67 at Expo '67 and the National Gallery of Canada in Ottawa?

A. Zaha Hadid
B. Moshe Safdie
C. Bruce Kuwabara

598. What Canadian singer-songwriter and musician was part of Buffalo Springfield in the 1960s, then became the fourth member of a renamed Crosby, Stills and Nash and has had huge solo successes as well?

A. Neil Young
B. Stephen Stills
C. Zal Yanofsky

599. Who starred as Captain Kirk on television from 1966 to 1969, as well as in seven movies, and is now often seen parodying himself in commercials?

A. Jim Carrey
B. William Shatner
C. Lorne Greene

WHAT IS CANADA?

ANSWERS 597–599

597. B. Moshe Safdie

Other works of Safdie include Vancouver Library Square; the main branch of the Salt Lake City Public Library; Kauffman Centre for the Performing Arts, Kansas City, Missouri; and the United States Institute of Peace, which is currently under construction in Washington, DC.

598. A. Neil Young

599. B. William Shatner

ART, LITERATURE AND ENTERTAINMENT

Questions 600 – 603

600. What actress was born and raised in Montréal and starred as Marie Antoinette in 1938, as Mary Hayes in *The Women* in 1939 and won the Academy Award for best actress in 1930 for her role in *The Divorcee*?
   A. Paulette Goddard
   B. Norma Shearer
   C. Mary Boland

601. What Canadian comedy duo had a series of comedy specials on CBC TV in the 1950s and appeared on *The Ed Sullivan Show* a record 67 times over 11 years?
   A. Abbot and Costello
   B. Gilles and Gillee
   C. Wayne and Shuster

602. What Québec-born innovator created and produced a series of silent films featuring inept policemen dubbed the "Keystone Cops"?
   A. Mack Sennett
   B. Charlie Chaplin
   C. Harold Lloyd

603. Who wrote the novel *St. Urbain's Horseman*, published in 1971?
   A. Margaret Atwood
   B. Morley Callahan
   C. Mordecai Richler

WHAT IS CANADA?

Answers 600 – 603

600. B. Norma Shearer
The classic film *The Women* was directed by George Cukor and also stars Rosalind Russell and Joan Crawford.

601. C. Wayne and Shuster

602. A. Mack Sennett
He was born in Richmond, Québec.

603. C. Mordecai Richler

THE DARK SIDE—CRIME, CRIMINALS, MISDEEDS AND MUCH MORE!

It's not all sunshine and lollipops up here in "The Great White North." But I'll bet you knew that. Enshrined in the Constitution Act of 1867 is the phrase "Peace, Order and Good Government." If we get nit-picky with this phrase, we all have to admit that we haven't always had "Good" government. So then, how accurate could the rest of that phrase be? Well, for the most part, I think it is probably accurate. And except for the over-reaching "Good Government" part, the rest of it is at least an ideal to which we aspire.

Aspirations inevitably imply that at times we have fallen short: massacres, rebellions, scandals, cheats, swindles, schemes, serial killers, exported media baron fraudsters, political assassinations, terrorists, religious cultists, lawmen gone bad, and even the wrongfully accused are all proof positive that things don't always go the way we wish they would. All of this fun will be found in this chapter of criminally devised questions and Canadian shenanigans, along with a few legendary lawmen as well.

604. In the late 19th and early 20th century, what area of canyons, gulches and buttes in southern Saskatchewan was stop number one on the outlaw trail, where famed outlaws such as The Sundance Kid, Dutch Henry, Coyote Pete, Sam Kelley (a.k.a. Charles "Red" Nelson), and the Pigeon Toed Kid fled to and hid out from the law?
   A. Castlerock
   B. The Chisholm Trail
   C. The Big Muddy Badlands

WHAT IS CANADA?

ANSWER 604

604. C. The Big Muddy Badlands

The Outlaw Trail was a series of trails and stopping places where America's Wild West outlaws could safely flee the law. The Big Muddy Badlands span the Saskatchewan-Montana border, so they were of particular use to outlaws who could do their deeds in the U.S. and quickly dash across the border to safe haven in Canada. The Big Muddy Badlands were the northern terminus of the Outlaw Trail that stretched across the U.S. to Mexico.

THE DARK SIDE—CRIME, CRIMINALS, MISDEEDS AND MUCH MORE!

QUESTIONS 605–607

605. What British-born Canadian actor portrayed police lieutenant Philip Gerard in the 1963–67 TV series "The Fugitive"?

A. Barry Morse
B. Lorne Greene
C. John Vernon

606. What Ontario town suffered a deadly outbreak of *E. coli* poisoning in 2000 that resulted in the deaths of seven people?

A. Waterdown
B. Walkerton
C. Welland

607. Which pair of murderers is known by various names, including the media-sponsored nicknames "The Ken and Barbie Murderers" and "The Schoolgirl Killers"?

A. Paul and Karla Bernardo
B. Colin Thatcher and Marc Carbonneau
C. Robert Pickton and Clifford Olson

ANSWERS 605 – 607

605. A. Barry Morse

He played the police officer hot on the trail of fugitive, Dr. Richard Kimball, played by David Janssen, who was in hot pursuit of the one-armed man.

606. B. Walkerton

Although town residents began complaining of problems on May 15, 2000, the public Utility insisted there was nothing wrong with the water supply. It was later discovered that the Utility was in possession of tests that had found evidence of contamination. It wasn't until May 21 that the medical officer of health warned the residents not to drink the water. Seven people died and 25,000 people fell ill due to the contaminated water supply. In the aftermath of the scandal, recommendations were implemented, but many, perhaps even most, people in the province blamed the cutbacks of the Ontario Conservative government for the tragedy.

607. A. Paul and Karla Bernardo

Their victims were Leslie Mahaffy, Kristen French and Karla's own sister Tammy. Paul Bernardo is serving multiple life sentences and has been declared a "Dangerous Offender," which means it is unlikely he will ever be released from prison. His ex-wife Karla Homolka (a.k.a. Karla Teale) was released from prison in 2005 thanks to a controversial deal she received for testifying against her ex-husband. She settled, at least for a time, in the Montréal area but apparently now lives in the Antilles in the West Indies and has a child. Many people believe that Karla is the much more dangerous of this murderous duo.

THE DARK SIDE—CRIME, CRIMINALS, MISDEEDS AND MUCH MORE!

QUESTIONS 608 – 609

608. What notorious bank robber and gang leader escaped from Toronto's Don Jail along with Lennie and Willie Jackson on November 14, 1951, and a second time with Steve Suchan and Lennie Jackson on September 8, 1952?
  A. Rocco Perri
  B. Edwin Alonzo Boyd
  C. Evelyn Dick

609. Who was captured, convicted and executed for the political assassination of Thomas D'Arcy McGee in 1868?
  A. Pearl Taylor
  B. Billy Miner
  C. Patrick James Whelan

608. B. Edwin Alonzo Boyd

Boyd became sort of a folk hero in Canada, owing to his rather gentlemanly ways when robbing banks. When he returned from serving in World War II, he drove a streetcar but quit that job to rob banks. He got caught and was sent to Toronto's Don Jail, where he met Lennie Jackson and Willie Jackson (not related). Soon after, they joined up with Valent Lesso (a.k.a. Steve Suchan) and the four began robbing banks. They pulled off one of the biggest robberies in Toronto history at the time. Newspapers dubbed them "The Boyd Gang," because they thought Boyd had to be the brains of the operation.

After Willie Jackson was arrested, Boyd went into hiding. In March 1952, Toronto police pulled over Lennie Jackson and Suchan, a gun battle took place and Suchan killed Detective Sergeant Edmund Tong. The two men escaped but were eventually captured and sent back to the Don Jail. A short time later Boyd was arrested and sent to the same jail. The three bank robbers again escaped. The biggest manhunt in Canadian history ensued, and 10 days later the gang was recaptured. Boyd received eight life sentences, and Willie Jackson got 30 years. In 1952, Suchan and Lennie Jackson were both hanged for killing Detective Tong. Boyd and Willie Jackson were released from prison in 1996. Boyd moved to BC and drove a bus for the disabled. The exploits of Boyd and his gang have been the subject of books and movies.

609. C. Patrick James Whelan

His ghost is said to still haunt the old Carlton County Jail where he was hanged. The jail is now the Ottawa Youth Hostel. There is some evidence to suggest that Whelan did not kill Thomas D'Arcy McGee and that as a Fenian sympathizer, he was used as a scapegoat. Whelan professed his innocence until the day he died.

THE DARK SIDE—CRIME, CRIMINALS, MISDEEDS AND MUCH MORE!

Questions 610–612

610. Five members of what Canadian-Irish family were murdered by their neighbours near Lucan, Ontario, on the night of February 4, 1880?
   A. The Donnellys
   B. The O'Connors
   C. The Valeras

611. Marc Carbonneau was part of what terrorist group that kidnapped British Trade Commissioner James Cross on October 5, 1979?
   A. FLQ
   B. Rhino Party
   C. Al-Quaida

612. Canadians in which of the following groups are most likely to be the victims of a crime?
   A. Males 18–24
   B. Males 25–59
   C. Females 30–39

610. A. The Donnellys

Although the Donnellys were hardly innocents, they were brutally murdered by their neighbours as a result of a longstanding feud in Biddulph Township, north of London, Ontario. The five Donnellys who died that night in 1880 were James and Johanna (mother and father), Tom (son), Bridget (cousin) and John Donnelly. Despite an eyewitness to the murders, no one was ever convicted for the deed.

611. A. FLQ (Front de Liberation du Québec)

Carbonneau, along with Louise Lanctot, Jacques Cossette-Trudel, Jacques Lanctot, Yves Langlois and Nigel Hamer, held James Cross for two months. Eventually Cross was released, and Carbonneau and the other terrorists were given safe passage to Cuba. With help from Québec's Parti Québecois, Marc Carbonneau returned to Canada and was sentenced to 20 months in jail, which he served.

612. A. Males 18–24

The remaining top five groups most likely to be victims of crime in Canada are:
- Males 25–29
- Males 30–39
- Males 40–49
- Males 50–59
- Females 30–39 (women in this age group are sixth most likely to be victims of crime and the most likely female group to suffer from criminal activities)

THE DARK SIDE—CRIME, CRIMINALS, MISDEEDS AND MUCH MORE!

QUESTIONS 613–615

613. Bernard Lortie was a member of the FLQ cell that kidnapped and murdered what Québec Labour Minister in October 1970?

A. Bernard Landry
B. Guy Paul Morin
C. Pierre Laporte

614. Which of the following is the most common type of crime in Canada?

A. Assault (including murder)
B. Theft under $5000
C. Fraud

615. In 1734, Portuguese-born black slave Marie-Joesph Angelique may have been wrongly executed for setting a fire that destroyed much of what city in New France?

A. Québec
B. Montréal
C. Tadoussac

613. C. Pierre Laporte

Three members of the FLQ (Bernard Lortie, Paul Rose and Francis Simard) were eventually convicted of the murder of Pierre Laporte. A fourth member of the group, Jacques Rose, was convicted of being an accessory after the fact.

614. B. Theft under $5000

The top 10 criminal offences in Canada (per 100,000 people) are:
- Theft Under $5000—2131
- Mischief—1107
- Break and Enter—860
- Assaults (level 1, 2, 3, excluding homicide and attempted murder)—732
- Other—695
- Motor Vehicle Theft—531
- Counterfeiting Currency—500
- Disturbing the Peace—366
- Bail Violations—327
- Fraud—304

(Courtesy Statistics Canada, 2004)

615. B. Montréal

Community sentiment was that Angelique had set fire to her master's home and it spread to much of Montréal. Although evidence was non-existent except for a questionable eyewitness account by a child, Angelique was convicted. She was then tortured (as was the custom back then) to try to induce her to confess (which she did, but who wouldn't after having their legs crushed by "the boot" and being beaten) before she was hanged.

THE DARK SIDE—CRIME, CRIMINALS, MISDEEDS AND MUCH MORE!

QUESTIONS 616–617

616. Where did a mass-murderer born with the name Gamil Gharbi kill 14 women and wound 10 women and men in Montréal on December 6, 1989?
   A. McGill University
   B. Olympic Stadium
   C. École Polytechnique

617. Convicted of three counts of mail fraud and one count of obstruction of justice, what disgraced former media baron goes by other monikers, including "Lord Black of Crossharbour" and "Inmate 18330-424"?
   A. Conrad Black
   B. Conrad Black
   C. Conrad Black

ANSWERS 616 – 617

616. C. École Polytechnique

Although the son of Algerian immigrants was born Gamil Gharbi, he is better known as Marc Lépine. The women whose lives he took were:

- Geneviève Bergeron (b. 1968), civil engineering student
- Hélène Colgan (b. 1966), mechanical engineering student
- Nathalie Croteau (b. 1966), mechanical engineering student
- Barbara Daigneault (b. 1967), mechanical engineering student
- Anne-Marie Edward (b. 1968), chemical engineering student
- Maud Haviernick (b. 1960), materials engineering student
- Maryse Laganière (b. 1964), budget clerk in the École Polytechnique's finance department
- Maryse Leclair (b. 1966), materials engineering student
- Anne-Marie Lemay (b. 1967), mechanical engineering student
- Sonia Pelletier (b. 1961), mechanical engineering student
- Michèle Richard (b. 1968), materials engineering student
- Annie St-Arneault (b. 1966), mechanical engineering student
- Annie Turcotte (b. 1969), materials engineering student
- Barbara Klucznik-Widajewicz (b. 1958), nursing student

617. A, B and C

We all know the bitter con by the name of Conrad Black, so I figured there was no sense in providing variant choices.

THE DARK SIDE—CRIME, CRIMINALS, MISDEEDS AND MUCH MORE!

QUESTIONS 618–620

618. Which Canadian province or territory has the highest per capita rate of crime (not including traffic offences)?
   A. Ontario
   B. British Columbia
   C. Northwest Territories

619. Who was wrongly accused and convicted of the murder of Saskatoon nursing assistant Gail Miller and wrongly incarcerated for that crime for almost 23 years?
   A. Guy Paul Morin
   B. David Milgaard
   C. Donald Marshall

620. What former Saskatchewan MLA was convicted and sent to jail for his involvement in the murder of his ex-wife JoAnn Wilson?
   A. Colin Thatcher
   B. Clifford Olson
   C. Bernard Ebbers

618. C. Northwest Territories

The list of provinces and territories by their rates of crime (per 100,000 people; excluding traffic offences) are:
- Northwest Territories—42,126
- Nunavut—36,685
- Yukon—23,125
- Saskatchewan—15,159
- Manitoba—12,753
- British Columbia—12,522
- Alberta—10,390
- Nova Scotia—8764
- Prince Edward Island—8220
- New Brunswick—7313
- Québec—6493
- Newfoundland and Labrador—6320
- Ontario—5702

(Courtesy Statistics Canada, 2004)

619. B. David Milgaard

620. A. Colin Thatcher

JoAnn Wilson divorced Thatcher in 1980. She was found murdered in 1983. Thatcher was tried and convicted for the murder in 1984 and was paroled in 2006.

THE DARK SIDE—CRIME, CRIMINALS, MISDEEDS AND MUCH MORE!

QUESTIONS 621–622

621. Which of Canada's major cities has the highest crime rate?

   A. Toronto
   B. Vancouver
   C. Winnipeg

622. Which of Canada's minor cities has the highest crime rate?

   A. Regina
   B. Saskatoon
   C. Halifax

621. C. Winnipeg

Canada's major cities as listed by their crime rates, from highest to lowest (counted per 100,000 people), are:
- Winnipeg—12,167
- Vancouver—11,814
- Edmonton—11,332
- Montréal—8173
- Calgary—7101
- Hamilton—5764
- Ottawa—5663
- Québec City—4997
- Toronto—4669

(Courtesy Statistics Canada, 2004)

622. A. Regina

Canada's minor cities according to their crimes rates (highest to lowest, with rates listed per 100,000 people) are:
- Regina—15,430
- Saskatoon—13,767
- Abbotsford—13,252
- Victoria—10,309
- Halifax—9924
- Thunder Bay—9226
- Windsor—7676
- London—7335
- St. John—7056
- Kingston—7010

(Courtesy Statistics Canada, 2004)

THE DARK SIDE—CRIME, CRIMINALS, MISDEEDS AND MUCH MORE!

QUESTIONS 623–625

623. Which wrongfully accused man is the son of the grand Chief of the Mi'kmaq Nation and spent 11 years in jail for a crime he did not commit?

A. Steven Truscott
B. Guy Paul Morin
C. Donald Marshall

624. Former armed forces corporal Denis Lortie killed three government employees while storming what province's National Assembly in 1984?

A. Québec
B. Newfoundland and Labrador
C. Manitoba

625. Founder of a spiritual community near Nanaimo, BC, in the 1920s, British mystic Edward Arthur Wilson is better known by which moniker?

A. HAL 19
B. Andre 3000
C. Brother XII

623. C. Donald Marshall

Donald Marshall Jr. was the wrongfully accused man; his father is Donald Marshall Sr. The younger Marshall was sentenced to life imprisonment for the stabbing death of Sandy Seale in Sydney, Nova Scotia, in 1971. The real murderer was Roy Ebsary, but the police and the rest of the justice system seemed bent on proving Marshall was the culprit.

624. A. Québec

On May 7, 1984, Lortie entered the Québec National Assembly building around 9:45 AM carrying two submachine guns. In the rampage, he killed Georges Boyer, Camille Lepage and Roger Lefrançois and also wounded 13 others. National Assembly's Sergeant-at-Arms, René Jalbert, emerged as a hero during this awful day in Canadian and Québec history. Jalbert spoke with Lortie, persuaded him to let the civilian hostages go and got him to go to his office. He also convinced him to surrender to military police, which he did at 2:22 PM. Jalbert was awarded the Cross of Valour by the Canadian government a few months later. In December 1995, Lortie was paroled from prison. Yikes!

625. C. Brother XII

He was born in Birmingham, England, in 1878, and he claimed to be the reincarnation of the Egyptian God, Osiris. His mistress, Mabel Skottowe, went by the name of Madame Z. Brother XII became increasingly dictatorial at the colony until a revolt broke out. A member of the colony escaped and told authorities at Nanaimo about what was going on. Brother XII destroyed the colony in a rage. He and Madame Z escaped authorities by tugboat. He is thought to have died in Switzerland in 1934, though there is some evidence that he faked his death.

THE DARK SIDE—CRIME, CRIMINALS, MISDEEDS
AND MUCH MORE!

QUESTIONS 626–627

626. Which Canadian province or territory has the highest rate of homicide (most killings per capita population)?

A. Ontario
B. Yukon
C. Alberta

627. What Canadian folk hero is sometimes called The Outlaw of Megantic and was the focus of the longest manhunt in Canadian history in 1888–89?

A. Donald McLean
B. Donald Morrison
C. Keith Morrison

626. B. Yukon

Yukon, with a homicide rate of 22.43 per 100,000 people, has the highest rate of homicide in Canada. The list for the country is as follows:
- Yukon—22.43
- Nunavut—13.49
- Northwest Territories—9.34
- Manitoba—4.27
- Saskatchewan—3.92
- Alberta—2.69
- British Columbia—2.67
- Ontario—1.51
- Québec—1.47
- Nova Scotia—1.39
- New Brunswick—0.93
- Newfoundland and Labrador—0.39
- Prince Edward Island—0

(Courtesy Statistics Canada, 2004)

627. B. Donald Morrison

He was born to Scottish immigrants near Lac Megantic, Québec. Donald's father was cheated out of the family farm by Lieutenant Colonel Malcolm MacAulay. Morrison was not content to sit by and just let that happen. He began to harass the new owners, and when their barn burnt down, he was blamed. A manhunt ensued. He was tried, sentenced to 18 years at hard labour, and eventually died as a result of TB.

THE DARK SIDE—CRIME, CRIMINALS, MISDEEDS AND MUCH MORE!

QUESTIONS 628–630

628. In 1959, at age 14, who was wrongfully accused of the death of Lynne Harper in Clinton, Ontario?
A. Steven Truscott
B. Guy Paul Morin
C. Walter Ostenak

629. Which province is number one when it comes to most homicides yearly?
A. Ontario
B. British Columbia
C. Prince Edward Island

630. What legendary Canadian lawman was born in Medonte Township, Upper Canada, was the third officer sworn in to the North-West Mounted Police (NWMP), was one of the NWMP officers who led the 1874 March west, and was responsible for leading his men in defeating Big Bear's forces in the last battle of the North-West Rebellion at Loon Lake?
A. Sam Houston
B. Sam Steele
C. Sam Lawrence

628. A. Steven Truscott

As a result of a trial, Truscott became the youngest person in Canadian history to be sentenced to death. His death sentence was commuted to life in prison, and he was released from prison in 1969. It took until August 2007 for Truscott to finally be acquitted of the charges by the Ontario Court of Appeal.

629. A. Ontario

With a total of 187 homicides in 2004, Ontario wins the dubious honour of most killings over the span of a year (2004). The breakdown across the country for the number of homicides in 2004 go thusly:

- Ontario—187
- British Columbia—112
- Québec—111
- Alberta—86
- Manitoba—50
- Saskatchewan—39
- Nova Scotia—13
- New Brunswick—7
- Yukon—7
- Northwest Territories—4
- Nunavut—4
- Newfoundland and Labrador—2
- Prince Edward Island—0

(Courtesy Statistics Canada, 2004)

630. B. Sam Steele

THE DARK SIDE—CRIME, CRIMINALS, MISDEEDS AND MUCH MORE!

QUESTIONS 631–633

631. What legendary figure of America's Old West had stints as a buffalo hunter, U.S. Army Scout, gambler, gunfighter, frontier lawman, sports editor for the *New York Morning Telegraph* and was born in November 1853 in Henryville, Québec?
   A. Bat Masterson
   B. Buffalo Bill Cody
   C. Wyatt Earp

632. Which major Canadian city has the highest rate of homicide?
   A. Edmonton
   B. Winnipeg
   C. Vancouver

633. Who was wrongfully accused of the October 1984 murder of his neighbour, Christine Jessop, and in 1992 wrongfully convicted of the crime after two trials?
   A. Evelyn Dick
   B. Rocco Perri
   C. Guy Paul Morin

631. A. Bat Masterson

He was born on either November 24 or 27, 1853, though no one knows for sure except perhaps his maker. Masterson served as a deputy alongside Wyatt Earp in Dodge City, Kansas. Although he was born Bartholomew Masterson, he later used the name William Barclay Masterson. Being one of the earliest of American spin doctors and a shameless self-promoter, names were certainly a fluid commodity to Bat, who was definitely shrewd and not at all batty! He died in New York City in 1921.

632. B. Winnipeg

With a homicide rate of 4.89 per 100,000 people, Winnipeg wins for having the highest homicide rate in 2004 for a major Canadian city. Across the country for major cities, the list breaks down thusly:

- Winnipeg—4.89
- Edmonton—3.39
- Vancouver—2.58
- Calgary—1.91
- Toronto—1.80
- Montréal—1.73
- Ottawa—1.14
- Hamilton—1.30
- Québec City—0.84

(Courtesy Statistics Canada, 2004)

633. C. Guy Paul Morin

DNA tests later proved that Morin had nothing to do with Christine Jessop's murder, and an inquiry uncovered evidence of wrongdoing and misconduct on the parts of the police and prosecution.

THE DARK SIDE—CRIME, CRIMINALS, MISDEEDS AND MUCH MORE!

QUESTIONS 634–635

634. Which of Canada's minor cities has the highest homicide rate?
- A. Abbotsford
- B. Kitchener
- C. Regina

635. What Alberta-born businessman founded WorldCom and was convicted of fraud and conspiracy in the largest (to date at least) accounting scandal in U.S. history?
- A. Jeffrey Skilling
- B. Bernard Ebbers
- C. Franklin Turtletaub

634. C. Regina

Regina has both the highest homicide rate for a minor city in Canada in 2004 and the highest for any city in Canada. The rest of Canada's minor cities' homicide rates in 2004 break down as follows:

- Regina—4.98
- Abbotsford—4.39
- Saskatoon—3.30
- Halifax—2.37
- Oshawa—1.82
- St. Catharines-Niagara—1.62
- Victoria—1.51
- Saguenay—1.35
- Kitchener—1.26
- Windsor—1.21

(Courtesy Statistics Canada, 2004)

635. B. Bernard Ebbers

And who said Canadians can't make it big in the United States. The biggest accounting scandal in U.S. history is definitely making it big! Ebbers, who was born in Edmonton in 1941, is currently serving a 25-year prison term in Louisiana for the convictions, which amounted to an $11 billion loss to investors. He is Inmate 56022-054 at the federal prison in Oakdale, Louisiana.

THE DARK SIDE—CRIME, CRIMINALS, MISDEEDS AND MUCH MORE!

QUESTIONS 636 – 637

636. What Canadian-born evangelist started her own newspaper, *The Bridal Call*, abandoned her husband, founded the Foursquare Church and then disappeared and re-appeared under dubious circumstances in 1926, leading to Obstruction of Justice charges?
   A. Aimee Semple McPherson
   B. Sister Sharon
   C. Elmer Gantry

637. What American-born stagecoach robber probably originated the phrase "hands up," was known for his politeness and staged Canada's first-ever train robbery in British Columbia on September 10, 1904?
   A. Rocco Perri
   B. Bill Miner
   C. Billy the Kid

636. A. Aimee Semple McPherson

She was born Aimee Elizabeth Kennedy in Salford, Ontario, in 1890 and was raised under strong Christian beliefs. On May 18, 1926, Aimee disappeared. She re-emerged 34 days later, claiming that she'd been kidnapped. Aimee and her mother were charged with Obstruction of Justice over the incident, but charges were eventually dropped because of lack of evidence. Aimee died in 1944 surrounded by a half empty bottle of Seconal (a sedative). Aimee's Foursquare Gospel Church continues on, though 90 percent of its members live outside the U.S. Aimee's son Rolph led the church for 44 years after her death.

637. B. Bill Miner

That first-ever Canadian train robbery was at Silverdale, 30 kilometres south of Vancouver. Miner was eventually arrested after an aborted train robbery near Kamloops. He served time in the BC Penitentiary, though after his release he returned to the U.S. where he was involved in more robberies and served more time in jail. The tale of his life was turned into a Canadian film (and a good one) in 1983 called *The Grey Fox* and stars Richard Farnsworth as Miner, and Jackie Burroughs as his girlfriend, photographer and feminist Katherine Flynn. The film was written by John Hunter and directed by the late and great Phillip Borsos.

THE DARK SIDE—CRIME, CRIMINALS, MISDEEDS AND MUCH MORE!

QUESTIONS 638 – 639

638. What Italian-born swindler worked for a bank in Montréal, served time in a Québec jail for cheque fraud and was the originator of an illegal get-rich-quick scheme that saw thousands of Americans swindled in 1920?
- A. Charles Ponzi
- B. Rocco Perri
- C. Vito Corleone

639. Which Canadian city had the most number of homicides in 2004?
- A. Montréal
- B. Toronto
- C. Vancouver

638. A. Charles Ponzi

The Ponzi Scheme is named for this rather inept swindler and is basically a pyramid scheme. Many of these are quite popular on the Internet today. So watch out and know anything that seems too good to be true, is! Ponzi pleaded guilty to mail fraud (a federal offence), was sentenced to five years and served 3.5. When he was released, he faced state charges and was sentenced to nine more years. He jumped bail and moved to Florida where he tried to swindle more gullible people by selling "prime real estate" that wasn't so prime. People were wise to him much sooner this time, and he fled to Texas and tried to flee the country. He was caught and sent back to Massachusetts where he was imprisoned until 1934. He eventually ended up in Brazil, and he died in poverty in 1948 after more attempted swindles here and there.

639. B. Toronto

With 94 homicides in 2004, Toronto tops the country for actual number of homicides. The top 10 Canadian cities according to their actual number of homicides in 2004 are:
- Toronto—94
- Montréal—63
- Vancouver—56
- Edmonton—34
- Winnipeg—34
- Calgary—20
- Ottawa—10
- Regina—10
- Halifax—9
- Hamilton—9

(Courtesy Statistics Canada, 2004)

THE DARK SIDE—CRIME, CRIMINALS, MISDEEDS AND MUCH MORE!

QUESTIONS 640–642

640. What former prime minister received an apology from the Canadian government as well as a $2.1 million award for the "Airbus Affair" in 1997, but admitted in 2007 before the Commons Ethics Committee to receiving hundreds of thousands of dollars from German-Canadian businessman Karlheinz Schreiber?

   A. Joe Clark
   B. Kim Campbell
   C. Brian Mulroney

641. In 1946, what Hamilton, Ontario woman was sentenced to hang for the death and dismemberment of her husband and was later convicted of manslaughter in the death of her infant son?

   A. Evelyn Dick
   B. Mabel Tilbury
   C. Belle Starr

642. What former civil servant was found guilty of defrauding the federal government and sentenced on June 19, 2006, to 42 months in jail for his part in the "Sponsorship Scandal"?

   A. Jean Chrétien
   B. Jacques Parizeau
   C. Charles Guité

Answers 640–642

640. C. Brian Mulroney

Because he was prime minister, he can be referred to as The Right Honourable Brian Mulroney. Although I like to refer to him as "Big Bri, the Manila Envelope Guy!"

641. A. Evelyn Dick

John Dick's dismembered torso was discovered by five children playing on the side of what Hamiltonians call "The Mountain," but is more accurately and less colloquially known as the Niagara Escarpment. Eventually, John's wife Evelyn and two men were charged with his murder. Evelyn was sentenced to hang for the murder, but the verdict was overturned on appeal. She was later convicted of the death of her infant son, whose body police had found while investigating the death of John Dick. The infant's body was found in the attic of Evelyn's home, encased in cement in a suitcase. Evelyn was sentenced to life in prison for the manslaughter of her son. She was paroled in 1958, and where she is now is anyone's guess.

642. C. Charles Guité

THE FIRST NATIONS

The intelligence, depth, culture, creativity and resourcefulness of the First Nations people are spread across what is now called Canada in a myriad of configurations, groups and at times conflagrations. They deserve their own chapter because of all that I've already said and because Europeans and Canadians misunderstood them and have been treating them badly since our first encounter.

There are some amazing people to be found among the First Nations, so here ya go, questions and answers dedicated to the first Canadians whose ancestors took those tentative steps across a land bridge in the north and made two continents their own... until we stole it from them!

643. What First Nations leader became a Cree chief at age 24, led his warriors to many victories, but was finally defeated by the Blackfoot in 1870?
  A. Pontiac
  B. Piapot
  C. Tecumseh

644. In what province is Head-Smashed-in Buffalo Jump, which has been designated a UNESCO World Heritage Site?
  A. Alberta
  B. Saskatchewan
  C. Manitoba

643. B. Piapot

The son of a Cree mother and Assiniboine father (both died of smallpox), Piapot and his grandmother were captured by the Sioux and lived with them until they were freed by a Cree war party many years later. Piapot was an able warrior and chief of the Cree, though at age 54 that came to an end with the defeat of his people near Fort Whoop-Up. His people were placed on a reserve near Indian Head, Saskatchewan, but they did not do well there. Piapot pushed for and got a better deal for his people that had them move to the Qu'Appelle Valley where living and hunting conditions were much better for them. By not joining the North-West Rebellion in 1885, Piapot shrewdly ensured government protection for his people.

644. A. Alberta

It is also a museum of Native culture.

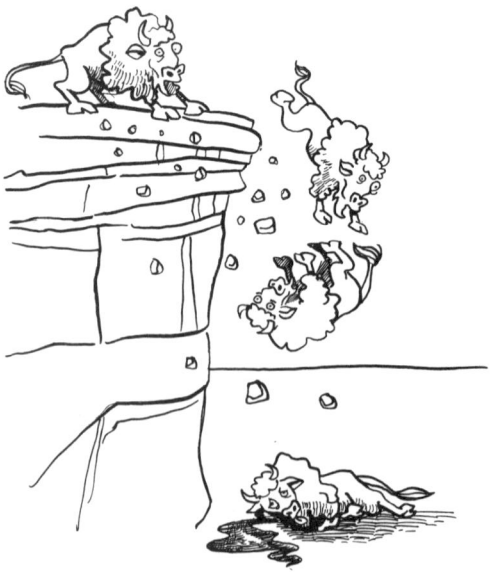

THE FIRST NATIONS

QUESTIONS 645 – 648

645. What bovine mammal was central to the lifestyle of plains First Nations people and nearly hunted to extinction by Europeans by 1879?

A. Grizzly bear
B. Moose
C. North American bison

646. How many First Nations people starved to death in the Northwest Territories between 1880 and 1885 because Lieutenant-Governor Edgar Dewdeney cut rations to reduce government costs despite guarantees outlined in treaties?

A. 3000
B. 30,000
C. 100,000

647. What traditional festival and ceremony practiced among First Nations people of the Pacific Northwest was strictly banned by the Canadian government for many years and involves the redistribution of wealth?

A. Koha
B. Moka
C. Potlatch

648. In what year were all First Nations people granted the right to vote in federal elections?

A. 1935
B. 1947
C. 1960

ANSWERS 645 – 648

645. C. North American bison

646. A. 3000

Because the bison had disappeared, most First Nations groups who agreed to treaties negotiated in them guarantees of food and help to begin farming.

647. C. Potlatch

Ceremonies and festivals vary widely among different peoples, but the essence of the potlatch is the same. Potlatch may involve feasts, music, dance and spiritual ceremonies celebrating births, weddings, funerals or rights of passage, such as moving from puberty into adulthood.

648. C. 1960

Native Americans in the United States had been given the right to vote in 1920.

THE FIRST NATIONS

QUESTIONS 649–652

649. In his 1969 White Paper, what Minister of Indian Affairs and future prime minister proposed abolishing Canada's Indian Act, rejecting Aboriginal land claims and assimilating First Nations people into the Canadian populace as "Other ethnic minorities," not as a distinct group?
   A. Pierre Trudeau
   B. Paul Martin
   C. Jean Chrétien

650. In 1981, who became the first "Treaty Indian" to be elected as a provincial politician in Canada?
   A. Phil Fontaine
   B. Elijah Harper
   C. Georges Erasmus

651. Known as Thayendanegea to his people, what Mohawk leader was a British military officer during the American Revolution?
   A. Joseph Brant
   B. Cornplanter
   C. Pontiac

652. What Ohsweken-born Six Nations actor was nominated for an Oscar for playing Kicking Bird in the 1990 film *Dances with Wolves* and had a recurring role as Edgar K.B. Montrose on *The Red Green Show*?
   A. Chief Dan George
   B. Tom Jackson
   C. Graham Greene

Answers 649–652

649. C. Jean Chrétien

First Nations groups vehemently opposed the White Paper's proposals, and the Liberal government of Pierre Trudeau quickly backed away from them.

650. B. Elijah Harper

He was elected to the Manitoba legislature and later gained national fame when he held an eagle feather as he refused to accept the Meech Lake Accord.

651. A. Joseph Brant

During the American Revolution, Brant saw action in a number of battles, including Oriskany and Cobleskill. In the ensuing peace treaty between the Americans and British, the Six Nations' land was awarded to the Americans despite pre-war promises to the contrary by British. Half of the Six Nations stayed on their lands in New York, while the other half moved to lands granted them by the British along the Grand River, which is now in Ontario.

652. C. Graham Greene

THE FIRST NATIONS

QUESTIONS 653–656

653. What land dispute between the Mohawk Nation and a Québec town began on July 11, 1990, and resulted in three deaths?
A. Ipperwash Crisis
B. Gustafsen Lake Standoff
C. Oka Crisis

654. On April 2, 1885, what Alberta community was attacked by Wandering Spirit and other Cree warriors resulting in the death of a hated Indian Agent named Thomas Quinn?
A. Duck Lake
B. Frog Lake
C. Frog's Leg

655. What is the Algonquin word for "spirit," "God" or "mystery"?
A. Manitou
B. Mississippi
C. Kinkajou

656. Known as Akay-na-muka, or Many Guns, who was Canada's first Native senator?
A. James Bartleman
B. James Gladstone
C. Bryan Trottier

653. C. Oka Crisis

It lasted for two months and was the result of a disputed land claim by the Kanesatake Mohawk involving a burial ground, and sacred trees, where the town of Oka wanted to build a golf course.

654. B. Frog Lake

In some circles, this attack is known as the Frog Lake Massacre, because after Quinn's death, the Cree warriors shot at settlers, killing nine people and taking three as captives. Wandering Spirit was eventually captured and hanged at Battleford, Saskatchewan, in November 1885.

655. A. Manitou

656. B. James Gladstone

He was born at Mountain Hill in the North-West Territories in 1887 and was a member of the Blood tribe of the Blackfoot Nation. He was appointed to the Senate on February 1, 1958. He died in British Columbia in 1971.

THE FIRST NATIONS

Questions 657 – 659

657. What constitutional amendment package was negotiated in 1987 without any input from Canada's Aboriginal peoples and was ultimately rejected through a national referendum?
A. Charlottetown Accord
B. Meech Lake Accord
C. Stornoway Accord

658. The Queen Charlotte Islands have been inhabited by which Native group for more than 6000 years?
A. Algonquin
B. Cree
C. Haida

659. What Métis leader studied to become a priest, was head of the provisional government of Red River, was an elected member of Canada's Parliament, suffered a nervous breakdown and was committed to an insane asylum, taught school in Montana, became an American citizen, joined the Republican party and was eventually hanged for treason for his part in the North-West Rebellion?
A. The Mad Trapper
B. Louis Riel
C. Jay Silverheels

ANSWERS 657 – 659

657. B. Meech Lake Accord

658. C. Haida

659. B. Louis Riel

After his nervous breakdown, Riel became less stable and more religiously devout. He thought he was "The Prophet of the New World." After his conviction, three doctors examined him to determine whether he was insane. Two of them thought he was sane. The official report of the doctors did not reflect their differing opinions. The federal Cabinet did not get the true opinions of the three doctors and decided Riel should be hanged. It is hard to say whether knowledge of a split opinion by the doctors would have changed the Cabinet's decision. Riel was hanged in Regina on November 16, 1885. His body is buried at the cemetery at the cathedral in St. Boniface, Manitoba.

QUESTIONS 660–662

660. What First Nations actor was born in British Columbia in 1899, appeared as Old Antoine on CBC's *Cariboo Country* in 1960 and was nominated for an Academy Award for playing Old Lodge Skins in the 1970 film *Little Big Man*?
   A. Jay Silverheels
   B. Chief Dan George
   C. Tom Jackson

661. What Chief of the Plains Cree attempted to prevent the violence and death at Frog Lake in 1885, and ultimately was tried and sentenced to prison because of the so-called Frog Lake Massacre?
   A. Big Bear
   B. Little Dear
   C. Gabriel Dumont

662. What national body represents the First Nations in Canada?
   A. National Indian Council
   B. League of Indians in Canada
   C. Assembly of First Nations

660. B. Chief Dan George

Born on July 24, 1899, in North Vancouver, BC, Chief Dan George was originally named Tes-wah-no and later known as Dan Slaholt. He spent most of his working life not as an actor, but in jobs ranging from longshoreman to construction worker. He also appeared in many other films, including *The Outlaw Josie Wales, Harry and Tonto* and *Americathon*. He died in British Columbia in September 1981.

661. A. Big Bear

He was sentenced to three years at Stony Mountain Penitentiary, but he was released before completing the sentence because of ill health. He died soon after, in 1888.

662. C. Assembly of First Nations

It formed out of the National Indian Brotherhood, which was founded in 1968, and became the Assembly of First Nations (AFN) in 1982. AFN was organized with the intent of being accountable to all First Nations in Canada.

THE FIRST NATIONS

QUESTIONS 663 – 666

663. What Métis-Canadian hockey player was born in Val Marie, Saskatchewan, and played 18 years in the NHL on six Stanley Cup–winning teams?
A. Mike Bossy
B. Bryan Trottier
C. Butch Goring

664. What Iroquois chief allowed Jacques Cartier to take two of his sons back to France in 1534?
A. Donnacona
B. Stadacona
C. Hochelaga

665. Blackfoot (Siksika), Blood (Kainai) and what other tribe make up the Blackfoot Nation?
A. Peigan
B. Sioux
C. Water

666. Mohawk, Oneida, Onondaga, Cayuga and Seneca were the five original First Nations groups that made up what Confederacy?
A. Blackfoot Nation
B. Iroquois Confederacy
C. Wendat People

663. B. Bryan Trottier

As an NHL player, he won six Stanley Cup rings with the New York Islanders and two with the Pittsburgh Penguins. He also has another Stanley Cup victory to his credit as an assistant coach with the Colorado Avalanche. Trottier also won the Conn Smythe Trophy, Hart Trophy, Art Ross Trophy, Calder Trophy and the King Clancy Memorial Trophy.

664. A. Donnacona

He didn't have much choice in the matter, because Cartier had seized Donnacona's sons, Domagaya and Taignoagny. Although Cartier returned Donnacona's sons unharmed, he again seized them, and Donnacona himself, among others, and took them all back to France. Donnacona died there, probably of disease.

665. A. Peigan

Peigan is also known as the Pikuni.

666. B. Iroquois Confederacy

THE FIRST NATIONS

Questions 667 – 670

667. What First Nations Shawnee leader helped Sir Isaac Brock force the surrender of Detroit in August 1812 and was killed at the Battle of the Thames in October 1813?
   A. Geronimo
   B. Pontiac
   C. Tecumseh

668. What Alberta-born, First Nations architect designed the Regina campus building of The First Nations University of Canada?
   A. Bruce Kuwabara
   B. Douglas Cardinal
   C. Arthur Erickson

669. What Haida artist sculpted the "Spirit of Haida Gwaii" for the Canadian Embassy in Washington, DC?
   A. Charles Edenshaw
   B. Robert Davidson
   C. Bill Reid

670. Who is the author of the play "Dry Lips Oughta Move to Kapuskasing," which premiered at Toronto's Theatre Passe-Muraille in 1989?
   A. Tomson Highway
   B. Billy Merasty
   C. Drew Hayden Taylor

667. C. Tecumseh

The Battle of the Thames took place near modern-day Chatham, Ontario. The British and First Nations force was defeated in the battle by American forces led by future president William Henry Harrison.

668. B. Douglas Cardinal

He is of Métis and Blackfoot heritage.

669. C. Bill Reid

670. A. Tomson Highway

The play is focused on seven men from a fictional reserve in northern Ontario. It's a companion piece to Tomson Highway's earlier play, "The Rez Sisters," which was about seven women from the same fictional community. Tomson Highway is a Cree playwright, novelist and children's author who was born in Brochet, Manitoba.

Questions 671–673

671. What was the sixth tribe to join the Iroquois Confederacy?
   A. Tuscarora
   B. Cree
   C. Huron

672. What discredited and condemned system tried to assimilate young First Nations into white, British culture through schools operated by churches?
   A. Residential school system
   B. Separate school system
   C. Public school system

673. In 1970, the Ontario government closed the commercial fishery run by the First Nations near what Ontario town because of severe mercury poisoning?
   A. Cornwall
   B. Niagara Falls
   C. Dryden

671. A. Tuscarora

When they joined the Iroquois Confederacy, the Five Nations became known as the Six Nations.

672. A. Residential school system

The first schools were set up in the 1600s by Roman Catholic missionaries, and the last of these abusive institutions was closed in the 1990s.

673. C. Dryden

The mercury poisoning was a caused by Dryden Chemical Company's waste-eater effluent that was allowed to be discharged into the Wabigon-English River. The local First Nations people were not only out of work, but also out of food, because the local fish had made up much of their diet.

THE POST-CONFEDERATION HISTORY OF CANADA

You've done it, friends. You've reached the final grouping of questions! And a fine way to finish, I do believe. This chapter contains all the post-Confederation brouhahas, politics, politicians of note and the biggest things that have happened in our 141 years as a country—or reasonable facsimile, thereof.

Have a read, have a think and, heck, go so far as to have a drink…while you're whiling away your time having the most fun of your life wading through the highs, lows and really low blows of Canada's first century and a half…in question-and-answer form, that is. The questions and answers await!

674. **On what date did the Dominion of Canada come into being?**
   A. May 24, 1867
   B. July 1, 1867
   C. July 4, 1867

675. **Which member of Alberta's "Famous Five" women was a magistrate and wrote under the pen name Janey Canuck?**
   A. Emily Murphy
   B. Nellie McClung
   C. Irene Parlby

Answers 674 – 675

674. B. July 1, 1867

675. A. Emily Murphy

Questions 676–679

676. Which of the following was *not* one of Canada's first four provinces?
A. Nova Scotia
B. New Brunswick
C. Prince Edward Island

677. Which former colony became two provinces at the time of Confederation in 1867?
A. Québec
B. Ontario
C. Canada

678. In 1880, who became Canada's first world title holder when he won the World Championship of singles rowing?
A. Jim Thorpe
B. Ned Hanlan
C. Freddy McBean

679. Which gold rush began when George Washington Carmack, Skookum Jim and Tagish Charlie discovered gold on Bonanza Creek in 1896?
A. Klondike Gold Rush
B. Cariboo Gold Rush
C. Fraser River Gold Rush

676. C. Prince Edward Island

677. C. Canada
Upper Canada and Lower Canada were merged into the single Province of Canada after the rebellions of 1837, with Canada East the former Lower Canada and Canada West the former Upper Canada. At the time of Confederation in 1867, the former Province of Canada became the two new provinces of Ontario and Québec.

678. B. Ned Hanlan
Edward (Ned) Hanlan defeated an Australian rower to take the championship on the Thames River course in England.

679. A. Klondike Gold Rush
Bonanza Creek was a tributary of the Klondike River. Some 100,000 fortune hunters headed to the Klondike to seek their fortunes between 1897 and 1899.

QUESTIONS 680–683

680. In 1909, what future prime minister became Canada's first minister of labour?
  A. Sir Wilfrid Laurier
  B. William Lyon Mackenzie King
  C. Louis St. Laurent

681. Which of Canada's prime ministers was born in Compton, Québec, in 1882?
  A. Sir Wilfrid Laurier
  B. Louis St. Laurent
  C. Lester B. Pearson

682. Who was Canada's prime minister during the first half of the 1930s and our only prime minister to date who was born in New Brunswick?
  A. Sir Robert Borden
  B. William Lyon Mackenzie King
  C. R.B. Bennett

683. In 1907, what fast-maturing wheat, which is well suited to Canada's Prairies, was developed by Charles Saunders?
  A. Buckwheat
  B. Marquis wheat
  C. Cream of wheat

680. B. William Lyon Mackenzie King

681. B. Louis St. Laurent

682. C. R.B. Bennett
Born at Hopewell Hill, New Brunswick, in 1870, he was Canada's 11th prime minister.

683. B. Marquis wheat
By 1920, Marquis wheat had become so popular with farmers that it made up 90 percent of the wheat grown on Canada's Prairies.

684. In 2000, who became the first female Chief Justice of the Supreme Court of Canada?
A. Beverley McLachlin
B. Louise Arbour
C. Nellie McClung

685. In 1976, who became the first Parti Québecois premier of Québec?
A. Robert Bourassa
B. Jacques Parizeau
C. René Lévesque

686. What was the last province to join Canada?
A. Newfoundland
B. Prince Edward Island
C. Manitoba

687. In what year were women given the right to vote in federal elections in Canada?
A. 1918
B. 1919
C. 1929

688. In December 1921, who became the first woman elected to Canada's House of Commons?
A. Adelaide Hoodless
B. Agnes Macphail
C. Emily Murphy

WHAT IS CANADA?

Answers 684 – 688

684. A. Beverley McLachlin

685. C. René Lévesque

686. A. Newfoundland
It joined Canada in 1949.

687. A. 1918

688. B. Agnes Macphail
She was the only woman elected to Parliament that year, which was the first federal election in which women could vote.

QUESTIONS 689–692

689. In February 1942, which ethnic group did the Canadian government announce would be removed from their homes in the coastal regions of British Columbia and relocated inland?
A. German
B. Italian
C. Japanese

690. What former journalist and liberal MP was sworn in as Canada's first female governor general in May 1984?
A. Adrienne Clarkson
B. Jeanne Sauvé
C. Michaëlle Jean

691. Who led the fight for women's suffrage in Québec, and in 1951 became leader of the provincial CCF party?
A. Emily Murphy
B. Thérèse Casgrain
C. Madame Duplessis

692. Who was prime minister of Canada during the Québec Referendum vote in 1980?
A. Joe Clark
B. Pierre Trudeau
C. Jean Chrétien

WHAT IS CANADA?

ANSWERS 689 – 692

689. C. Japanese
More than 20,000 men, women and children of Japanese origin were sent to detention camps in the interior of British Columbia or to farms in Alberta and Manitoba. Their properties were also sold off.

690. B. Jeanne Sauvé

691. B. Thérèse Casgrain

692. B. Pierre Trudeau

693. Which prime minister's unpopular trade policies helped cause his electoral defeat in 1911?
A. Sir Wilfrid Laurier
B. Sir Robert Borden
C. Charles Tupper

694. In 1998, which former federal Conservative became leader of Québec's Liberal party?
A. Jean Charest
B. Jean Chrétien
C. Lucien Bouchard

695. To date, who is the only former premier of Nova Scotia to become prime minister of Canada?
A. Lester B. Pearson
B. John Diefenbaker
C. John Thompson

696. Which political party, founded on August 1, 1932, in Calgary, was led by J.S. Woodsworth?
A. Liberal Party
B. CCF
C. Social Credit Party

697. Which Canadian province was the last to give women the right to vote?
A. Québec
B. Manitoba
C. Ontario

Answers 693–697

693. A. Sir Wilfrid Laurier

694. A. Jean Charest

695. C. John Thompson
Thompson was a Conservative and served as prime minister from 1892 to 1894. He died of heart failure while dining at Windsor Castle in England.

696. B. CCF
Its official name was the Co-operative Commonwealth Federation.

697. A. Québec
Women in Québec finally got the right to vote in 1940.

698. In what British Columbia locale was the "Last Spike" driven for the Canadian Pacific Railway on November 7, 1885?
   A. Craigellachie
   B. Kamloops
   C. 100 Mile House

699. What bitter, seven-week-long strike began on May 15, 1919?
   A. St. John Harbour Seal Strike
   B. Winnipeg General Strike
   C. Hamilton Stelco Strike

700. Which Canadian prime minister was born in Berlin, Ontario?
   A. Sir John Abbott
   B. William Lyon Mackenzie King
   C. Sir John Thompson

701. In 1905, which Canadian prime minister created the provinces of Alberta and Saskatchewan?
   A. Sir Wilfrid Laurier
   B. R.B. Bennett
   C. Alexander Mackenzie

Answers 698–701

698. A. Craigellachie
The last spike was hammered in by Donald Smith, a supporter and financial backer of the railway who became Lord Strathcona.

699. B. Winnipeg General Strike

700. B. William Lyon Mackenzie King
Berlin changed its name to Kitchener during World War I, for obvious reasons.

701. A. Sir Wilfrid Laurier

Questions 702–706

702. In 1989, who became Canada's first female combat soldier?
- A. Debra Gray
- B. Sheila Copps
- C. Heather Erxleben

703. Who was Canada's first Liberal prime minister?
- A. Alexander Mackenzie
- B. Mackenzie Bowell
- C. Sir Charles Tupper

704. What funny-money political party, led by William "Bible-Bill" Aberhart, won Alberta's general election in 1935?
- A. NDP
- B. Green Party
- C. Social Credit

705. In 1948, who succeeded William Lyon Mackenzie King as prime minister?
- A. Lester B. Pearson
- B. John Diefenbaker
- C. Louis St. Laurent

706. In 1870, what became the first new Canadian province created after Confederation?
- A. British Columbia
- B. Saskatchewan
- C. Manitoba

ANSWERS 702–706

702. C. Heather Erxleben

703. A. Alexander Mackenzie
He was prime minister from 1873 to 1878 and was preceded and succeeded by Sir John A. Macdonald.

704. C. Social Credit

705. C. Louis St. Laurent
He was Canada's 12th prime minister and served from 1948 to 1957.

706. C. Manitoba

THE POST-CONFEDERATION HISTORY OF CANADA

QUESTIONS 707–710

707. What tariff agreement went into effect on January 1, 1989?
   A. GATT
   B. Free-Trade Agreement
   C. Hosing of Canada Agreement

708. In 1930, who was sworn in as Canada's first female senator?
   A. Jeanne Sauvé
   B. Cairine Wilson
   C. Bertha Wilson

709. Woodside National Historic Site is the boyhood home of what wartime Canadian prime minister?
   A. Sir Robert Borden
   B. Stephen Harper
   C. William Lyon Mackenzie King

710. Who became Newfoundland's premier one day after the province joined Canada?
   A. Brian Peckford
   B. John Crosby
   C. Joey Smallwood

WHAT IS CANADA?

Answers 707–710

707. B. Free-Trade Agreement
It was later expanded through NAFTA.

708. B. Cairine Wilson
She was born in Montréal in 1885 and died in Ottawa in 1962.

709. C. William Lyon Mackenzie King
It is in Kitchener, Ontario.

710. C. Joey Smallwood

Questions 711–713

711. In 1992, who became the first Canadian woman in space?

A. Roberta Bondar
B. Sally Ride
C. Julie Payette

712. In 1911, who succeeded Sir Wilfrid Laurier as prime minister?

A. Alexander Mackenzie
B. Arthur Meighen
C. Sir Robert Borden

713. On June 25, 1993, who became Canada's first female prime minister?

A. Kim Campbell
B. Jeanne Sauvé
C. Sheila Copps

Answers 711–713

711. A. Roberta Bondar
She was also the second Canadian astronaut in space.

712. C. Sir Robert Borden

713. A. Kim Campbell
She served less than five months as prime minister and only six months as Conservative Party leader.

NOTES ON SOURCES

Abbott, Elizabeth, ed. *Chronicle of Canada*. Montréal, QC: Chronicle Publications, 1990.

Brooks, Tim, and Earl Marsh. *The Complete Directory of Primetime, Network and Cable TV Shows*. New York, NY: Ballantine Books, 2003.

The Calgary Herald.

Colombo, John Robert, ed. *Penguin Dictionary of Popular Canadian Quotations*. Toronto, ON: Penguin Canada, 2006.

Crystal, David, ed. *The Cambridge Biographical Encyclopedia*. Cambridge, UK; New York, NY: Cambridge University Press, 1995.

de Figueiredo, Dan. *Weird Canadian Places*. Edmonton, AB: Blue Bike Books, 2005.

———. *Weird Ontario Places*. Edmonton, AB: Blue Bike Books, 2006.

———. *Canadian Top 10 Lists*. Edmonton, AB: Blue Bike Books, 2007.

———. *Fakin' Eh! How to Pretend to be a Canadian*. Edmonton, AB: Blue Bike Books, 2007.

Douglas, Ann. *The Complete Idiot's Guide to Canadian History*. Scarborough, ON: Prentice Hall, Canada Inc., 1997.

The Encyclopedia of Animals. San Francisco, CA: Frog City Press, 1993.

Fazakas, Ray. *The Donnelly Album*. Toronto, ON: MacMillan of Canada, 1977.

Glazer, Stephen. *Random House Word Menu*. New York, NY: Random House, 1997.

The Globe and Mail.

Grun, Bernard. *Timetables of History*. New York, NY: Simon & Schuster, 1991.

Harrowsmith Country Life Magazine.

Hay, Peter. *MGM: When the Lion Roars*. Atlanta, GA: Turner Publishing Inc., 1991.

Hirsch Jr., Ed, Joseph F. Kett, and James Trefill. *The Dictionary of Cultural Literacy*. Boston, MA: Houghton Mifflin Company, 1993.

The Holy Bible, King James Version.
Leacock, Stephen. *Canada: The Foundations of Its Future.* Montréal, QC: Privately Printed, 1941.
Louda, Jiri, and Michael Maclagan. *Heraldry of the Royal Families of Europe.* New York, NY: Clarkson N. Potter Inc. Publishers, 1981.
Merriam-Webster's Encyclopedia of Literature. Springfield, MA: Merriam-Webster, Incorporated, 1995.
Merriam-Webster's Geographical Dictionary. 3rd ed. Springfield, MA: Merriam-Webster, Incorporated, 1998.
Michaelides, Marina. *Bathroom Book of Alberta Trivia.* Edmonton, AB: Blue Bike Books, 2006.
Murphy, Angela. *Bathroom Book of Canadian Trivia.* Edmonton, AB: Blue Bike Books, 2005.
The New York Public Library Desk Reference. 2nd ed. New York, NY: Prentice Hall General Reference, 1993.
The Ottawa Citizen.
The Oxford Complete Dictionary of Quotations. 3rd ed. Oxford, UK; New York, NY: Oxford University Press, 1980.
Pevere, Geoff, and Greig Dymond. *Mondo Canuck: A Canadian Pop Culture Odyssey.* Toronto, ON: Prentice Hall Canada, 1996.
Pound, Richard W. *Canadian Facts and Dates.* 3rd ed. Markham, ON: Fitzenry & Whiteside, 2005.
Russo, Vito. *The Celluloid Closet.* New York, NY: Harper & Row Publishers, 1987.
Thay, Edrick. *Weird Canadian Words.* Edmonton, AB: Folklore Publishing, 2004.
Thomas, Dave. *SCTV: Behind the Scenes.* Toronto, ON: McClelland & Stewart Inc., 1996.
The Toronto Star.
The Toronto Sun.
Trager, James. *The People's Chronology.* New York, NY: Henry Holt and Company, 1994.
Watson, Patrick. *Canadians: Omnibus Edition.* Toronto, ON: McArthur & Company, 2002.
Wojna, Lisa. *Bathroom Book of Canadian Quotes.* Edmonton, AB: Blue Bike Books, 2005.

NOTES ON SOURCES

Websites

Atanarjuat, http://atanarjuat.com/

Margaret Atwood, http://www.owtoad.com/

Arthur Black, http://www.basicblack.com/

Britannica On-line http://www.britannica.com

The Canadian Encyclopedia, http://www.thecanadianencyclopedia.com

Canadian Forces, http://www.forces.gc.ca

Canadian Heritage Department, http://www.canadianheritage.gc.ca

CBC, http://www.cbc.ca

Governor General of Canada, http://www.gg.ca

http://www.histori.ca

Internet Movie Database, http://www.IMDB.com

Stephen Leacock, http://www.leacock.ca/

McGill University, http://www.mcgill.ca

Robert Munsch, http://www.robertmunsch.com/

Statistics Canada, http://www.statcan.ca

U.S. Federal Bureau of Prisons, http://www.bop.gov/iloc2/LocateInmate.jsp

Virtual Saskatchewan Online, http://www.virtualsk.com

ABOUT THE ILLUSTRATORS

Pat Bidwell

Pat has always had a passion for drawing and art. Initially self-taught, he completed art studies in Visual Communication in 1986. Over the years, he has worked both locally and internationally as an illustrator product designer and graphic designer, collecting many awards for excellence along the way. When not at the drawing board, Pat pursues other interests solo or with his wife, Lisa, such as landscaping, gardening, travelling, the symphony and the opera.

Roger Garcia

Roger Garcia is a self-taught artist with some formal training who specializes in cartooning and illustration. He is an immigrant from El Salvador, and during the last few years, his work has been primarily cartoons and editorial illustrations in pen and ink. Recently he has started painting once more. Focusing on simplifying the human form, he uses a bright minimal palette and as few elements as possible. His work can be seen in newspapers, magazines, promo material and on www.rogergarcia.ca

Patrick Hénaff

Born in France, Patrick Hénaff is mostly self-taught. He is a versatile artist who has explored a variety of media under many different influences. He now uses primarily pen and ink to draw and then processes the images on computer. He is particularly interested in the narrative power of pictures and tries to use them as a way to tell stories.

ABOUT THE ILLUSTRATORS

Graham Johnson

Graham Johnson is an illustrator and graphic designer. When he isn't drawing or designing, he... well...he's always drawing or designing! On the off-chance you catch him not doing one of those things, he's probably cooking, playing tennis or poring over other illustrations.

Peter Tyler

Peter is a recent graduate of the Vancouver Film School's Visual Art and Design and Classical animation programs. Though his ultimate passion is in filmmaking, he is also intent on developing his draftsmanship and storytelling, with the aim of using those skills in future filmic misadventures.

Roly Wood

Roly grew up in Indian River, Ontario. He has worked in Toronto as a freelance illustrator and was also employed in the graphic design department of a landscape architecture firm specializing in themed retail and entertainment design. In 2004, he wrote and illustrated a historical comic book set in Lang Pioneer Village near Peterborough. Roly currently lives and works as a freelance illustrator in Calgary, Alberta, with his wife, Kerri, and their dog, Hank.

ABOUT THE AUTHOR

Dan de Figueiredo

Dan de Figueiredo has written four previous books for Blue Bike—*Fakin' Eh! How to Pretend to Be a Canadian, Canadian Top 10 Lists, Weird Canadian Places* and *Weird Ontario Places*. By day he's a humour columnist, journalist and television writer. By night...well, you don't want to know. His love of words and ideas began when he received a copy of *Robinson Crusoe* at the age of seven, and he has never looked back. After earning a BA in Political Science at McMaster University, Dan earned a Journalism degree from Ryerson. In TV, he has written for the Canadian edition of *Who Wants to Be a Millionaire, TimeChase, Inside the Box* and *Cooler Facts*, and has been producer of *Reach for the Top*. Most recently he was head writer for the wacky Discovery Channel Quiz Show, *Cash Cab*. Dan has also written a number of plays and several independent films.